SAGE GROUSE

ICON OF THE WEST

SAGE GROUSE
ICON OF THE WEST

NOPPADOL PAOTHONG

Written By **KATHY LOVE**

Sponsors

Pat Jones

Zachary H. Shafran

Rudi Roeslein

Published by Laguna Wilderness Press
PO Box 5703
Laguna Beach, CA 92652-0149
Tel 951-827-1571
Email: orders@lagunawildernesspress.com
www.lagunawildernesspress.com
www.facebook.com/lagunawildernesspress

The Laguna Wilderness Press is a non-profit press dedicated to publishing books concerning the presence, preservation, and importance of wilderness environments.

5 4 3 2 1 21 20 19 18 17

ISBN: 978-0-9840007-3-9
Library of Congress: 2017950815

First Edition, January 2018
Design by Stephanie Thurber and Susan Ferber
Printed in China, Four Colour Print Group, Louisville, Kentucky

(Front cover) A male sage-grouse is in full breeding regalia in southern Idaho.
(Back cover) A male sage-grouse performs a spring courtship dance on the lek in predawn hours in the Red Desert, Wyoming.

Our task must be to free
ourselves by widening
our circle of compassion
to embrace all living
creatures and the whole
of nature and its beauty.

— Albert Einstein

Bone Draw Creek flows into the Big Sandy
River in Eden Valley, Wyoming.

The greatness of a nation
and its moral progress
can be judged by the way
its animals are treated.

—Mohandas K. Gandhi

Male sage-grouse gather on a lek just before
sunrise in Carbon County, Wyoming.

Contents

Journey to the West

Noppadol Paothong

ONE FROSTY SPRING MORNING MY FRIEND TOOK ME TO HIS favorite sage-grouse gathering area (lek) in Wyoming. He promised it would take my breath away. We sat in his vehicle on a hill overlooking the lek. It was five in the morning and still too dark to see our surroundings, but the familiar popping sounds made by males' air sacs resonated through the air.

As the sun rose over the horizon, casting a pink glow on a distant mountain peak and illuminating the valley below, I couldn't believe my eyes. More than 250 birds were performing their elaborate courtship display; it was the largest sage-grouse gathering I had ever seen. It was a sight that I will never forget. With little human interference and no manmade structure nearby, the birds were thriving here. Gazing at this endless horizon, I couldn't help but wonder

about the future of this place. That thought brought me deep sadness.

During the sixteen years I have worked with grassland grouse, I have seen populations disappear throughout their range. Several places where I have photographed grouse performing their courtship dance no longer have any birds. This has become a common occurrence due to rapid land conversion accelerated by the oil and gas boom.

The sage-grouse is a beautiful species of bird that makes its home in the Sagebrush Sea. Its spring courtship dance is one of the most flamboyant mating displays in nature. It easily captures the hearts of people who are fortunate enough to witness it. I tried to imagine the reaction of people who first came into contact with these birds. Were they in awe and as inspired by

the birds as I am? Explorers and settlers frequently encountered sage-grouse and even supplemented their diets with the birds. Many Native American tribes have revered sage-grouse for thousands of years and still honor the birds in their ceremonial dance and dress.

My first encounter with sage-grouse was in 2005 in southern Idaho. I was on a quest to photograph all North American grassland grouse for my book *Save the Last Dance*. When that project was finished in 2012, I was completely exhausted from my intensive eleven-year journey. I didn't realize that it was just the beginning of another journey.

A year later, while visiting with a friend in Wisconsin, I looked through his collection of hard-to-find bird books and ran into *The Sage Grouse in Wyoming* by Robert L. Patterson. It is based on his research on greater sage-grouse for the Wyoming Game and Fish Department in 1952. The book, the most comprehensive study of greater sage-grouse to this day, contains several incredible black-and-white photographs of sage-grouse taken by the author. While looking through the book, the image of a fearless hen guarding her nest in front of sagebrush caught my attention, not only because I had never seen an image of sage-grouse other than spring courtship, but also because it showed the spirit and behavior of the birds that I had yet to encounter. If someone like me, who's been documenting grouse for a long time, hasn't seen or known about this, I imagined that most people do not know about other aspects of these birds, either. So the idea of pursuing and documenting the sage-grouse life-cycle started to intrigue me.

To achieve my goal of documenting their life cycle would take me another five years, including many bone-chilling mornings in a photo blind, hiking in pitch darkness, and driving in terrain that resembles the moon. It isn't uncommon for the weather in the High Desert to turn from warm and sunny to a blinding blizzard in a matter of hours. Wildlife here have adapted to this harsh environment over millennia, and we are just newcomers to their home range.

Sage-grouse are symbols of this unique and diverse habitat of the North American West, but few people realize how much these birds depend on the health of this habitat to survive. To many, the High Desert may seem empty and desolate. In reality, it is home to abundant wildlife that rely on its unique ecosystem. Like the sage-grouse, they make their homes here and nowhere else.

In March of 2015 I took my then five-year-old daughter to northwest Missouri to see prairie chickens for the first time. A small remnant population remains there on undisturbed prairie and visitors are allowed to witness their courtship dance. It was a little after four in the morning when my family and I hiked to a blind. I heard excitement in my daughter's voice as she looked up in the sky where the Milky Way cast its magic over a cloudless sky. "How many stars do you see?" I asked. Her answer was earnest. "Too many to count!" she replied. It startled me to think that she is one of very few kids to experience this. In fact, research shows that 80 percent of children in the U.S. have never seen a sky dark enough to see a starry night. As towns and cities continue

to grow and get brighter, natural darkness is becoming extremely rare. A study suggests that by 2070 most of the U.S. will be too bright to observe the night sky. Perhaps not coincidentally, these darkest places—without human development—are where sage-grouse flourish and thrive.

During my time spent in the field I met many conservationists, biologists, and ranchers who work diligently to protect these iconic birds and their fragile habitat. While their conservation methods may differ, their passion, dedication, and devotion to preserve the birds and the land of the West bring them together to work on a common goal.

My hope for this book is to introduce the beauty and spirit of sage-grouse and the land they depend on, and to increase awareness and the understanding of its value and dire plight. I also hope to deepen the discussion about conservation efforts. For these conservation efforts to be successful, they must be made in ways that will benefit all—humans and wildlife—that live in and near sage-grouse habitat.

Looking back to the morning I spent in the photo blind with my daughter, I remember the smile on her face as she watched prairie-chickens dancing at dawn. She was in awe of the beauty and spirit of the birds as they danced. Somehow I saw a glimpse of hope in her generation.

Nature has a way to teach us. It also has the incredible power of putting things in perspective. We can't force someone to care for nature; they have to appreciate it for themselves, whether from the experience of watching the sun rise over an ocean, listening to the songs of birds, or witnessing the bizarre yet spectacular displays of sage-grouse.

I hope that my images in this book will remind people of the places these birds call home—places that are truly beautiful and unique to the American West. Perhaps these spring dancers will inspire us all to care for them, the icon of the West.

It is rare to witness the gathering of hundreds of sage-grouse like this one in Wyoming, but it was a common sight in the 1800s when early explorers and settlers often encountered large flocks of the birds.

Introduction

Michael A. Schroeder

THE DATE WAS JUNE 5, 1805, AND MERIWETHER Lewis, William Clark, and their Corps of Discovery were near the confluence of the Marias and Missouri rivers in present-day Montana. The Corps of Discovery had just passed westward through the Great Plains, the vast, fertile grasslands that would eventually be cultivated into North America's breadbasket. The country that now opened before them was the Sagebrush Sea, more than a quarter million square miles of "emptiness" dominated by sagebrush that appeared to be largely toxic. Lewis wrote in his journal, "I saw a flock of the mountain cock, or a large species of heath hen with a long pointed tail which the Indians informed us were common to the Rockey Mountains, I sent Shields to kill one of them, but he was obliged to fire a long distance at them and missed his aim." These words begin the written history of sage-grouse, but they also tell us that the Mandan, with whom Lewis and his company had spent the previous winter, already knew about sage-grouse.

Sage-grouse have a prominent place in the history of the American West. Indigenous people revered these birds for their abundance as a food source, their dramatic appearance, and their exotic behavior. Some of this is reflected in traditional dances and art depicting the sage-grouse and in its unique name in the Shoshone language, *seedskadee* or *sisk-a-dee,* which is still used in Wyoming.

Lewis and Clark continued to write about sage-grouse in their journals, including a five-hundred-word description on March 2, 1806, that provided information about their distribution in the West, appearance, habitat, and behavior. Today one can read hundreds of published articles about sage-grouse and learn much specific information about their appearance, genetics, distribution, migration, food, habitats, breeding behavior, conservation, and management,

Meriwether Lewis sketched a sage-grouse in his journal to accompany his first description of the bird. *Photo courtesy of Missouri History Museum*

This depiction of a strutting sage-grouse was found on Anasazi pottery in Arizona.

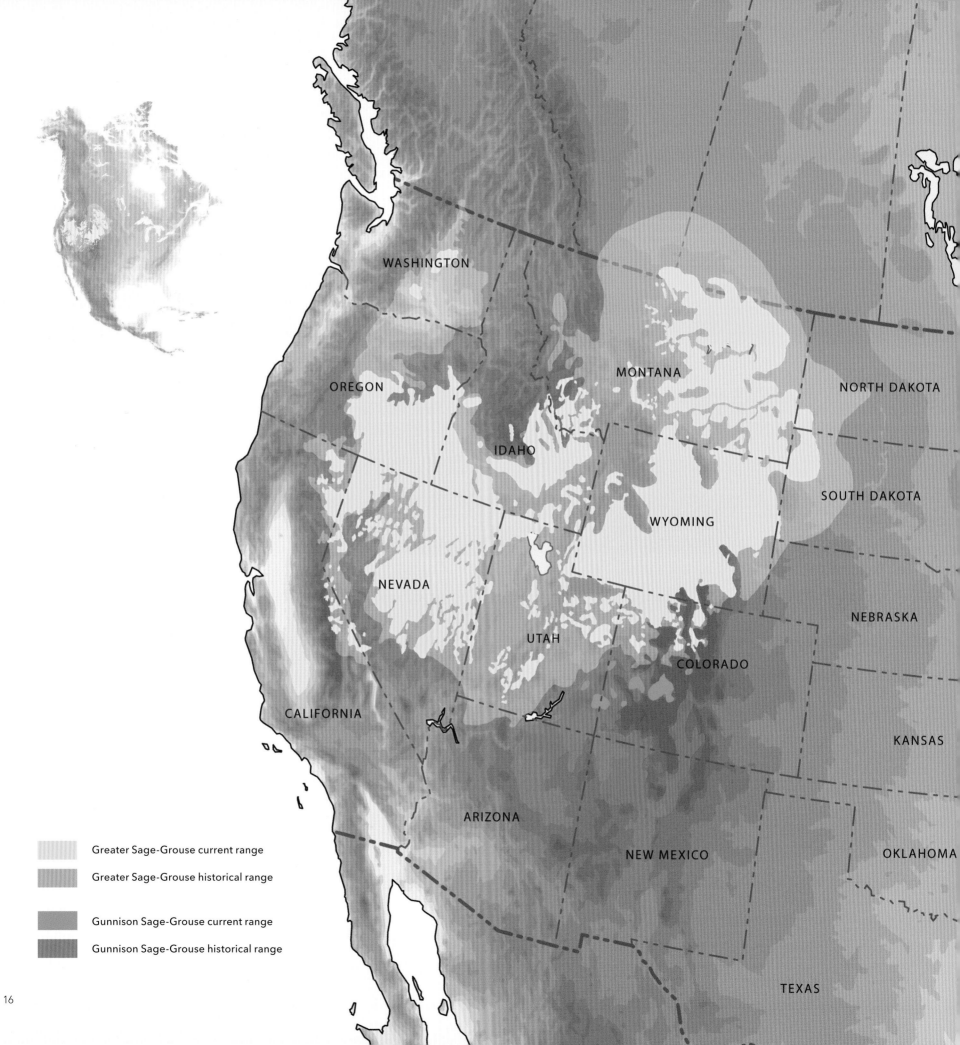

WASHINGTON

OREGON

MONTANA

NORTH DAKOTA

IDAHO

SOUTH DAKOTA

WYOMING

NEVADA

NEBRASKA

UTAH

CALIFORNIA

COLORADO

KANSAS

ARIZONA

NEW MEXICO

OKLAHOMA

TEXAS

Greater Sage-Grouse current range

Greater Sage-Grouse historical range

Gunnison Sage-Grouse current range

Gunnison Sage-Grouse historical range

but the essence of what makes sage-grouse both unique and interesting has been known for at least two centuries.

The birds' common names reflect our evolving knowledge about them, their habitat, and the plants associated with them; in addition to the original native names and the current common ones, "greater sage-grouse" and "Gunnison sage-grouse," they have been called "mountain cock," "cock of the plains," "sage hen," and "sage cock." For most of our written history, the greater sage-grouse (*Centrocercus urophasianus*) and the Gunnison sage-grouse (*Centrocercus minimus*) were considered indistinguishable, but in 2000 ornithologists determined that they were separate species differing in size, appearance, behavior, and genetics. Greater sage-grouse are larger and have less prominent filoplumes (the long feathers behind the head), and the males of the two species have different breeding displays. Gunnison sage-grouse are found only in Colorado and southeastern Utah. Even with these differences, however, there is nobody who would ever question that they belong to the same genus. This book focuses on the greater sage-grouse.

The Sagebrush Sea and sage-grouse are firmly intertwined in both history and biology. Sage-grouse depend on sagebrush for both food and cover. The two species of sage-grouse are among the few animals that can eat and thrive on the toxic leaves of sagebrush. In fact, a full-grown male greater sage-grouse can weigh more than seven pounds and represents the largest grouse species in North America. The species' dependence on sagebrush is so strong that its gizzard, unlike that of any other grouse species, lacks the musculature needed to digest hard foods like seeds. Meriwether Lewis noted that "the gizzard of it is large and much less compressed and muscular than in most fowls" and that "the food of this fowl is almost entirely that of the leaf and buds of the pulpy leafed" sagebrush. The only time of year that sage-grouse depart significantly from this diet is during the summer, when insects and vegetation such as the leaves and flowers of wildflowers are both abundant and palatable.

There are few areas where sage-grouse have made a greater name for themselves than that of breeding behavior. The breeding of sage-grouse is centered on and near traditional strutting grounds called leks. The typical strutting display of a male sage-grouse consists of slow walking accompanied by swishing noises produced as he rubs his wings briefly against his stiff, short breast feathers. This is followed by two

Every spring male sage-grouse gather on a lek and perform an elaborate display to attract female sage-grouse.

distinctive loud "plops" produced by the rapid expansion of large esophageal pouches underlying the bird's breast. The skin on the outside of these pouches is bare, so this behavior also produces a remarkable visual spectacle.

Males congregate on leks to display, fight, and breed with females. The pageantry and competition on leks is legendary, and scientists and naturalists have long been fascinated with the behavior. For example, a greater-sage grouse dominated the cover of the May 1978 issue of *Scientific American*, which featured an in-depth article on sage-grouse breeding behavior by the renowned animal behavior specialist R. Haven Wiley. Because only a few males do most of the breeding, research has often focused on which males are successful—the clean ones (having few parasites), the active ones (with rapid displays), the loud ones, or the dominant ones. A successful male may copulate with more than twenty females in a morning and more than a hundred times in a single breeding season, meaning that most males do not breed. The intense competition to be one of the successful males is perhaps one reason males are roughly twice the size of females.

Following copulation, females alone focus on nesting and brood rearing. During spring (March through May), they lay usually six to nine eggs in a shallow nest bowl on the ground; the nest is at least partially concealed by vegetation, usually under low cover of big sagebrush, to protect against weather and predators. In areas where sagebrush grows taller, other vegetation, such as perennial grasses, may also be important for cover. This dependence on sagebrush and grass is one reason sage-grouse are so impacted by overgrazing and wildfire. When the eggs hatch after about twenty-seven days of incubation by the female, the hen and her chicks will spend the next two to four months together in habitats relatively rich in wildflowers and insects. This nesting and brood-rearing period is a critical time for sage-grouse, and mortality of chicks can be high. Once sage-grouse are fully

Many Native American tribes throughout the West still honor sage-grouse in their ceremonial dances and dress.

grown, they generally have relatively high survival rates, even in harsh winters. Survival is particularly important to offset years when reproductive success is relatively low.

At the Smithsonian Institution in Washington, DC, there is a box containing the skeleton of a male sage-grouse that has the number 17972. What makes this specimen unusual? On November 16, 1886, this sage-grouse was one of many that flew to a spring near the headwaters of Big Porcupine Creek in eastern Montana, apparently to get a drink of water. As luck would have it, William Hornaday, chief taxidermist for the U.S. National Museum (now the Smithsonian), happened to be camped next to that spring, and he took full advantage of the collecting opportunity.

Hornaday was in Montana to collect bison before they became extinct. At that time, the estimated total population of bison scattered throughout Montana, Colorado, and Texas was believed to be about 250, mere remnants of the original herds of more than 20 million. Hornaday wrote, "In our eagerness to succeed in our task, the sad fact that we were hunting the last representatives of a mighty race was for the time being lost sight of." And succeed they did. In addition to the specimens they collected, they also brought back a live calf. It did not live long, but its short life produced a public relations miracle. One of the large bulls the expedition had shot became the model for what became the buffalo nickel. The result of this was increased public interest in conservation of wildlife, especially the bison. Hornaday's interest in sage-grouse paralleled his interest in bison. In 1916 he wrote an article on how to save the sage-grouse from extinction, asking, "Shall this fine bird follow the passenger pigeon into oblivion?"

Along with Hornaday, many others collected sage-grouse throughout the West in the pursuit of science, and these specimens are cataloged and stored in many museums. This scientific pursuit helped establish our knowledge of the historical distribution of sage-grouse from California to Colorado to Saskatchewan and British Columbia and most areas in between. The collections are supplemented with early observations. On June 6, 1826, David Douglas wrote that sage-grouse "are seen abundantly and are easily killed by the Indians with the bow on the banks of the Columbia from the junction of the Spokane River to the Walawallah [Walla Walla] River." This is consistent with what Meriwether Lewis wrote on March 2, 1806: "The cock of the plains is found in

The rugged terrain of the West (above) was a challenge to early settlers and gold rush prospectors of the 1800s. John and Metta Weston (right) were among the would-be farmers to settle in the area near Milford, Utah, around 1900.
Photo courtesy of Brad Weston

FOLLOWING PAGE

In a winter white-out, thousands of pronghorns roam freely across the High Desert. The vast open landscape of the Sagebrush Sea is often celebrated as the American Serengeti.

the plains of Columbia and are in great abundance." On June 30, 1834, near South Pass in present-day Wyoming, John Townsend wrote,

We have seen also another kind of game, a beautiful bird, the size of a half grown turkey, called the cock of the plains. We first met with this noble bird on the plains, about two days' journey east of Green river, in flocks, or packs, of fifteen or twenty, and so exceedingly tame as to allow an approach to within a few feet, running before our horses like domestic fowls, and not unfrequently hopping under their bellies, while the men amused themselves by striking out their feathers with their riding whips.

In 1892, Charles Bendire described an observation by George Grinnell six years earlier of a flock of sage-grouse near Bates Hole in central Wyoming: "There must have been thousands of them."

Duane Coombs, a rancher and coordinator for the Intermountain West Joint Venture, walks through a field of basin wild rye (*Leymus cinereus*) in the Nevada High Desert where he managed a cattle ranch.

Unfortunately, populations of sage-grouse have declined almost everywhere. The birds are no longer found in Arizona, Nebraska, and British Columbia, and populations are at risk of extirpation in North Dakota, South Dakota, Washington, Alberta, and Saskatchewan. Sage-grouse are being impacted by habitat conversion, landscape fragmentation, invasive plants, roads, transmission lines, oil wells, and overgrazing. None of these factors operates alone, so reversing the decline requires a multifaceted approach. But despite their problems, there are still good populations of sage-grouse in some core areas of the distribution: Colorado, Idaho, Montana, Nevada, Oregon, Utah, and Wyoming.

Representatives from the Western states first began discussing long-term conservation of sage-grouse in 1954. That early effort has expanded to include all states, provinces, and agencies that manage land within the sage-grouse distribution. This rangewide approach has produced numerous proactive management activities including development of conservation actions on private lands, compromises in grazing practices, improved fence designs, conservative harvest regulations, information sharing across jurisdictional boundaries, and reduced development pressure in identified sage-grouse core areas.

Some may question the wisdom and economics of conservation actions designed to save a single species. However, the sage-grouse is much more than a single species being impacted by land use. It shares the sagebrush ecosystem with species such as pronghorn, white-tailed jackrabbit, black-tailed jackrabbit, pygmy rabbit, Brewer's sparrow, sagebrush sparrow, sagebrush thrasher, ferruginous hawk, golden eagle, and northern harrier. When we protect the habitat for sage-grouse, we also protect it for the other species that depend on it. We humans also live in this habitat; we need its soil, its water, and its full, healthy ecosystem. For the good of sage-grouse and for our own well-being, we need to develop better ways to share.

At the same time, sage-grouse are a living part of our human heritage. They resonate through the history of the American West, from the Native Americans who depended on them to the experiences of settlers and the present-day bird watchers who travel great distances just to see sage-grouse. The sage-grouse is a beautiful, mobile, tough bird that reflects the wildness and expansiveness of its habitat. It thrives in an environment that can reach more than one hundred degrees

Wind farms and oil and gas development in sagebrush habitat add to the list of challenges to the birds and their survival: Wind farms in Carbon County, Wyoming (above) and oil and gas development in Jonah field, Wyoming (right).

Sage-grouse often thrive in winter as long as they find enough sagebrush and snow to provide food and water.

in the summer and forty degrees below zero in the winter, with unrelenting wind. A bird like this deserves our respect.

In the two centuries since Meriwether Lewis first wrote about sage-grouse, these birds have been a lightning rod for controversy. There have been disagreements about the impacts of harvest, livestock grazing, and energy development and also arguments about the need for federal conservation actions such as listing under the Endangered Species Act. In the case of federal listing, the U.S. Fish and Wildlife Service has vacillated between recommending listing and recommending not listing, the latter being the current approach. To further illustrate the diversity of opinion, most upland bird hunters treasure sage-grouse for the wildness of its habitat, the dramatic nature of the bird, and the uniqueness of the table fare when grouse is the main course. In contrast, John Townsend wrote on June 30, 1834:

> When we first saw them, the temptation to shoot was irresistible; the guns were cracking all around us, and the poor grouse falling in every direction; but what was our disappointment, when, upon roasting them nicely before the fire, we found them so strong and bitter as not to be eatable. From this time the cock of the plains was allowed to roam free and unmolested, and as he has failed to please our palates, we are content to admire the beauty of his plumage, and the grace and spirit of his attitudes.

Perhaps Townsend had a point. Despite the contradictions that sage-grouse engender, it is essential that we all recognize a basic truth. Sage-grouse belong in the sagebrush landscapes of western North America. Without this species, the landscape will have lost something vital to its essence, a wild link between the past and future, between Native Americans and present-day naturalists, and between pristine unmanaged landscapes and fenced rangelands. It is up to us to ensure that these links are never broken.

— Michael A. Schroeder, Ph.D,
Upland Bird Research Scientist,
Washington Department of Fish and Wildlife

A hen takes a dip into a pool of spring water during the hot summer in the High Desert of Wyoming.

During the peak of mating season, a large group
of hens will cluster around a dominant male
and even fight among themselves to be bred.

Sage-grouse belong in the sagebrush landscapes of western North America. Without this species, the landscape will have lost something vital to its essence, a wild link between the past and future, between Native Americans and present-day naturalists, and between pristine unmanaged landscapes and fenced rangelands. It is up to us to ensure that these links are never broken.

—Michael A. Schroeder

Gunnison sage-grouse are about one-third smaller than the greater, but have longer and thicker filoplumes. The males of the two species also exhibit different breeding displays: the Gunnison percolate nine times instead of the two of the greater sage-grouse and finish with a tail wag. Gunnison sage-grouse are found only in Colorado and southeastern Utah.

Gunnison Sage-Grouse

The Gunnison sage-grouse was acknowledged to be a distinct species of grouse in 2000, the first "new" bird species to be recognized in the U.S. since the 1800s.

There are fewer than 5,000 Gunnison sage-grouse in the wild now, concentrated in seven populations in southwestern Colorado and eastern Utah, with the largest population occurring in the Gunnison Basin of Colorado. The birds have been extirpated from Arizona, Kansas, New Mexico, and Oklahoma. They were listed as threatened under the Endangered Species Act in 2014. The usual suspects are responsible for the population decline: roads, energy development, cultivation, fences, power lines, subdivisions, grazing. The list goes on.

Jessica Young, professor of environmental management at Western State Colorado University, first recognized the distinctions between Gunnison grouse and greater sage-grouse by listening to recordings of their vocalizations during courtship. Young recalls,

In 1988, I was working on sage-grouse in the Sierra Nevadas as an undergraduate at the University of California-San Diego. We received a tape of vocalizations of the grouse in the Gunnison Basin. I listened to it and looked at the sonograms. Then I borrowed equipment from my professors, my father built me a blind, and my mother and I drove to Gunnison and to Northern Colorado to film grouse in both locations. The Gunnison grouse were distinctly different in behavior and sound, while the sage-grouse near North Park were indistinguishable from the ones I had studied in the Sierras in California.

The strut rate of the Gunnison sage-grouse was slower, and the birds "popped" their air sacs nine times compared to the greater sage-grouse's two pops. Other differences emerged in size, coloring, feathers, and genetics. One very visual difference is the filoplumes—the dark feathers that crown the head. Sage-grouse filoplumes are sparser and spread around the sides of the head, while the Gunnison's filoplume looks like a black pony tail on the back of the head.

Young determined that female Gunnison grouse avoided recorded mating vocalizations of greater sage-grouse and theorized that such aversion would prevent hybridization as an explanation for

Gunnison sage-grouse's mating calls sound like a percolator coffee pot, while the greater belches a gurgling "kerplunk."

the Gunnison population. Genetic, behavioral, and morphological testing confirmed they were a distinct species; Young and her colleagues published their findings in December, 2000.

"This is a landscape bird," said Young. "It specializes in using very small pieces of a very large landscape." Like greater sage-grouse, Gunnison sage-grouse have extreme "site fidelity"—they use the same breeding, nesting, and over-wintering sites year after year. When these areas are damaged or destroyed, the population that uses them will likely die off. This was dramatically illustrated in the 1960s when the Blue Mesa Reservoir was built in southern Colorado. The rising water inundated several leks. For the next few years, Gunnison grouse gathered on the ice over their leks, futilely performing their spectacular dance.

The
Open Book

The Sagebrush Sea represents the wide open
spaces beloved in the West. Once dominating
250 million square miles in eleven states,
development has shrunk it to half its original size.

The vast expanse of the Sagebrush Sea
surrounds a lone mule deer buck.

In the sagebrush lands of the West …
the natural landscape is eloquent of the
interplay of the forces that have created it.
It is spread before us like the pages of an
open book in which we can read why the
land is what it is and why we should preserve
its integrity. But the pages lie unread.

—Rachel Carson, *Silent Spring*

Sagebrush made its home in the Western landscape
35,000 years ago. Sage-grouse depend on this nutrient-
rich plant for their survival throughout the year.

RACHEL CARSON DESCRIBES THE NATURAL LANDSCAPE OF
America's sagebrush steppe as an open book that tells us "why the land
is what it is and why we should preserve its integrity." Carson "read" the
landscape and recognized that it harbored species and spaces that are iconic
symbols of the western United States. They should be preserved because they
are, in a word, beloved.

But before Carson wrote *Silent Spring* in 1962, before Lewis and
Clark recorded seeing sage-grouse in 1805, even before Native Americans
incorporated grouse into their lore and legends, the bird and the landscape
were coevolving into an integrated, interdependent network. Over millennia,
the sagebrush landscape shaped grouse, and grouse graced the landscape.

The quarter-million-square-mile sagebrush steppe of North America is now
half its original size. It once stretched unbroken across parts of eleven western
states, from eastern Washington to central Wyoming and south to Arizona
and New Mexico. It came to be known as the Big Empty, the Sagebrush Sea—
few trees, limitless horizons, a sky unbroken by the structures of man. But
within its seemingly harsh ecosystem, at least 297 species of birds, 87 species
of mammals, 63 species of fish, and countless species of reptiles and insects
flourish. Elk, pronghorn, mule deer, pygmy rabbits, American badgers, golden
eagles, northern harriers, coyotes, sagebrush lizards, and harvester ants are
among the creatures that find shelter and sustenance among the many species
of sagebrush and other plants that make up the Sagebrush Sea.

Big sagebrush (*Artemisia tridentata*), a tough, pungently aromatic shrub
in the sunflower family, dominates the flora of the Sagebrush Sea, but many
species and hybrids of *Artemisia,* plus hundreds of native grasses and forbs,
create a mosaic of habitats. The perennial bunchgrasses and wildflowers
complement the subtle sagebrush palette, and anchoring them all is a complex
web of soil overlain by green algae, brown algae, fungi, and lichens that serves
to stabilize the soil, retain moisture, and fix nitrogen.

Pollen records show that big sagebrush has been around for more than
thirty-five thousand years. It can be recognized by its grayish, wedge-shaped,
three-toothed leaves protected by silvery hairs, and its characteristic aroma:
astringent, with an odor of, yes, sage. It can reach a height of eight feet. It
flowers in late summer or early fall, with many small, yellow blossoms in long
clusters along its branches.

Sagebrush leaves contain bitter aromatic oils called terpenoids that make
the plant unpalatable to grazing cattle, motivating farmers and ranchers to try
to destroy it with herbicide and fire. But ranchers in dry areas see at least one
good side to sagebrush: it holds moisture that falls in the form of winter snow,
releasing it slowly into the soil as the snow melts. In bare areas, snow blows off
and snowmelt runs off without sinking into the soil.

Big sagebrush is well adapted to its harsh environment. It flourishes in dry
areas like the Great Basin, the heart of its range, where average precipitation is
just nine to twelve inches per year, thanks to characteristics that help it retain
moisture. Its stems and leaves have a waxy coating that protects them from the
scorching sun. Fine, dense hairs on the leaves reduce evaporation and reflect
sunlight, which helps the inner tissue retain water. When leaves fall to the
ground and decay, they emit a toxic substance that acts as a natural herbicide,
discouraging competing plants from invading its territory.

Sagebrush sparrow

Sage thrasher (eggs)

Pygmy rabbit

Sage-grouse depend on sagebrush, especially big sagebrush. They prefer habitat with between 10 and 30 percent sagebrush cover. They eat it, sleep in it, and nest under its sheltering branches. The birds have evolved special adaptations that enable them to use sagebrush to survive harsh conditions. For example, mature birds dine almost exclusively on the leaves of sagebrush, which retains its leaves even during bitter cold and deep snow. The birds possess a long middle toe that helps them dig through snow to reach the protein-packed leaves. Comblike extensions develop along their toes that function like snowshoes, helping them walk on top of the powdery blanket. In contrast to other gallinaceous birds (such as prairie-chickens and ruffed grouse), sage-grouse have an elongated, less muscular gizzard adapted to digesting leaves rather than tough grains and seeds.

One would think that these natural attributes and defenses might make sage-grouse and sagebrush superheroes of the Big Empty. But, as always, human forces have altered the landscape, changing the rules of the game for plants and animals. In the Columbia Plateau alone, more than 90 percent of sagebrush steppe has been plowed under. By the 1970s, more than five million acres of sagebrush had been destroyed by mechanical means, sprayed with herbicide, or burned to improve grazing. The total population of sage-grouse was once estimated at sixteen million or more, but it has plummeted to two hundred thousand to four hundred thousand birds. The loss of habitat has resulted in the disappearance of sage-grouse from areas such as British Columbia, Nebraska, and Arizona, and the plunder continues as the list of challenges to the birds and their habitat grows; fire, invasive plants, mining, oil and gas extraction, wind farms, fencing, power lines, grazing, and climate change all threaten to close the open book of the Sagebrush Sea.

Everything Is Connected

A small area of sagebrush—say, a few square meters—reveals a universe of diversity. There is Mother Sage Hen, hidden in the low brush atop a crude ground nest, incubating her eggs. Invertebrates such as harvester ants crawl nearby. (When the grouse eggs hatch, the chicks will eat the ants and other insects.) A pygmy rabbit tunnels among the sagebrush roots. A ferruginous

A small area of sagebrush reveals a universe of diversity. They all belong to the community that biologists call "sagebrush obligates." They must make their living in the stark environment between sagebrush and open sky.

hawk soars overheard, and a sagebrush lizard is safely camouflaged along the stout stems of big sagebrush. A hoof intrudes on the scene; it belongs to a pronghorn, grazing the sage and forbs before moving on with its herd. They all belong to the community that biologists call "sagebrush obligates." In other words, they must make their living in the stark environment between sagebrush and open sky.

Native Americans once worked in harmony with that landscape, relying on and often managing nature's bounty to nourish themselves physically and spiritually. Wilson Wewa is a spiritual leader known throughout the Great Basin, where he has led Native American religious ceremonies for forty years. He recalls his grandfather explaining to him when he was a young child that the strange clicking and popping noises they heard in the distance were from the mating dance of the sage-grouse.

Wewa has seen many sage-grouse mating grounds disappear from eastern Oregon during his lifetime. "They used to be plentiful, but they were pushed out by cattle, paved roads, logging roads, and hundreds of thousands of acres of cultivated oats and barley," he said. In an admonition especially relevant to human reliance on fossil fuels and the resulting climate change, he adds, "Everything is connected. Man's technology will not last forever. If we aren't careful, it will have a negative impact on the whole world."

Ferruginous hawk

Vesper sparrow

Sagebrush lizard

Sage-grouse were called *pi-imsh* by the Walla Walla tribes and *mak-esh-too-yoo* by the Nez Perce. Along the northern edge of their range the Crow called sage-grouse *sisk-a-dee,* and near the western edge the Washoe called them *see-yook.* Wewa's tribes, the Northern Paiute and Nez Perce, relied on grouse and other animals and plants to survive. They hunted them with nets and with bows and arrows. They made tea from sagebrush to cure stomach and eye ailments, and they burned it to purify the air for ceremonies. They wove sagebrush into cloth for shelter and clothes, and they wove the bird into myth and legend. The University of Oregon is publishing a book of their legends based on Wewa's recollections of the old tales.

Wewa has worked with tribal elders since 1980 as director of the senior center in Warm Springs, Oregon. He treasures his memories of the elders he met when he started the job; he called them "horse-and-buggy" seniors because they had witnessed the transformation from the traditional culture of past generations to the modern era of technology. "I learned from them and heard their stories. They had all passed by the 1990s," Wewa said. "But we [Native Americans] still have a connection to nature. We are born into it. We hunt, fish, dig roots, pick berries. In these ways we learn to work with nature, not against it."

Climate change is bringing warmer temperatures to central Oregon, attracting birds normally seen only as far north as Mexico; Wewa noted that it is also bringing fire ants and killer bees. Scientists believe climate change is also exacerbating fires, droughts, and nonnative species invasions at such a fast pace that the iconic plants and animals of the Sagebrush Sea will not be able to adapt. In 2011, the National Park Service conjectured that climate change could also encourage the spread of West Nile virus to birds in the region.

Fire and Lack of Fire

Christian Hagen, a grouse researcher on the faculty of Oregon State University-Corvallis, studies two of the many threats to sagebrush habitat, a pair that might be summed up, ironically, as fire and lack of fire. He leads two long-term projects to study the degree to which fire and its absence affect grouse habitat and how the consequences can be mitigated.

Wildfires occur naturally in the dry environment of the Sagebrush Sea and are usually set by lightning strikes. Native Americans intentionally burned small sections of land, perhaps to promote the growth of grass and forbs. But unchecked fires over broad swaths of land destroy the slow-growing sagebrush that grouse need for survival. Under certain conditions, a wildfire may remove tens of millions of acres of sagebrush habitat annually west of the Rockies.

Hagen began studying the results of a five-hundred-thousand-acre wildfire, the Holloway Fire, that occurred in southeastern Oregon and northeastern Nevada in 2012. "Given the scale of that fire, the grouse should have left the area. Instead, they remained and tried to eke out a living, but in many cases it cost them their lives," Hagen said. "Grouse have extreme site fidelity." Birds return to the same places where they conduct their annual mating dances year after year, and females nest within a few to a hundred yards of a previous year's nest. In the burned area, nest survival and adult survivorship dropped well below what was needed for a viable population. Lacking sagebrush for nourishment and shelter, the birds may have starved or fallen victim to predation.

The story of fire in the Sagebrush Sea is inextricably linked to cheatgrass (*Bromus tectorum*), an exotic invasive annual grass that made its appearance in the West around 1910. The resin-rich grass burns easily and frequently. When fire destroys the sagebrush, cheatgrass often takes over. "You can think of sagebrush as the 'old growth' of the basin," Hagen said. "It will take fifteen to twenty years to come back in more resilient sites or up to fifty where conditions are not ideal." Cheatgrass invades quickly and typically burns every two to three years from lightning strikes. When native vegetation is suppressed by fire, the cheatgrass establishes a monoculture that offers nothing to sage-grouse and other wildlife.

Wildfires allow cheatgrass to dominate native vegetation at drier, lower-elevation sites, but lack of fires at higher elevations creates conditions for juniper (*Juniperus occidentalis*) to invade. The branches of this tree provide perches for sage-grouse predators, and over time the invading trees will convert sagebrush to a juniper woodland that is simply unsuitable for grouse. Hagen calls these conditions that promote juniper and cheatgrass "the big squeeze" for sage-grouse populations.

"One saving grace is that the junipers are slow-growing, and the sagebrush undergrowth often remains intact for several years," he said. His study, begun in 2010, is showing that when thin stands of juniper are removed by hand-felling, the sagebrush habitat is restored and sage-grouse move into these areas quickly. "The results are very encouraging," Hagen said. "With millions of acres of sagebrush compromised by juniper encroachment, we now have a path forward to effectively address this threat to the species."

This arrowhead found on a sage-grouse lek in Wyoming is silent testimony to Native Americans' dependence on the bird over millennia.

Great Basin and the Life Within

The Great Basin comprises about two hundred thousand square miles of the Sagebrush Sea, primarily in Nevada and parts of western Utah. The name "Great Basin" was coined by the explorer John C. Fremont in the 1840s to denote its lack of connection to the sea. Geographers call these regions that lack outlet rivers that flow into a sea "endorheic basins." But rather than the single cup-shaped depression the word "basin" implies, the Great Basin is a series of more than ninety closed valleys ringed by mountains. Elevations range from below sea level to more than four thousand feet above it. The valleys retain the scant rainfall and spring runoff in seasonal riparian areas—narrow streams or large, flat playa lakes—that in most cases evaporate in late summer. Geologists believe the Great Basin was created over millennia when huge blocks of the earth's crust were uplifted, dropped, and tilted. The uplifted parts eroded over time, leaving behind stunning rock formations. Volcanic rock in

the basin reveals that it is more than thirty million years old.

Jay Tanner is a rancher in the Great Basin whose Mormon family migrated there in the 1870s. His great-grandmother was nineteen years old when she arrived in the remote area of northwestern Utah and noted that the primitive houses of early settlers "looked like cowsheds." But she stayed, married, and raised a family that has persisted and prospered in Grouse Creek Valley.

"There was a tremendous amount of grouse here when the settlers arrived," said Tanner. His great-grandfather raised sheep in the wide open spaces of the basin, but Tanner's generation relies on cattle. It takes a lot of land in the Great Basin to grow a cow; Tanner figures he needs forty acres per cow, on average, for a year's growth. His landholdings number in the tens of thousands of acres, and he leases several hundred thousand acres more from the Bureau of Land Management, the federal agency that manages most of the land that makes up the Sagebrush Sea.

Tanner feels an affinity for sage-grouse. He likes to see their spectacular dance and leads groups of visitors to his ranch to view grouse on their nearby strutting grounds, the leks. He likes the birds' connection to his family heritage in Grouse Creek Valley and the fact that they are one of at least 350 wildlife species at home on his land. But he has also come to realize, as a rancher who depends on his land for his livelihood, that "what's good for the bird is good for the herd." Managing his land to benefit sage-grouse also promotes quality cattle.

When junipers took over about nine thousand acres of Grouse Creek Ranch, squeezing out sagebrush and native grasses so that neither grouse nor cattle could use the land, Tanner took action. Under a program with the Natural Resources Conservation Service, which paid three-quarters of the cost, he systematically removed the junipers over the course of several years. He and his crew used different methods to remove the trees, depending on the site, including chainsaws, chains, crawlers, and excavators, and reseeded the cut areas with grasses and forbs. "It was amazing to see the transformation," Tanner said. "The sage-grouse came back almost immediately. It was a tremendous success story, and it helped every other sagebrush-loving creature, too, such as mule deer."

The Last Dark Places

Tanner and Hagen have read the "open book" of the Sagebrush Sea that Rachel Carson noted and come to the same conclusion about why it should be preserved.

"The Great Basin is one of the last great dark places in the Lower Forty-Eight," said Hagen. When viewed from a satellite, most areas of the planet are alight with cities, towns, and other human development.

Vast, unbroken space is needed if sage-grouse and associated species are to endure. Sage-grouse need diverse resources during their life cycle—open stages on which to breed, secure cover for nesting, riparian areas, and, above all, vast

The sagebrush sea should be preserved in order to maintain many species that depend on it, including humans. The interests of ranchers and scientists overlap in a single iconic species: the sage-grouse.

vistas of sagebrush. Because the availability of these resources varies in both space and time, large, intact landscapes are necessary for this highly mobile species. You can have the most pristine sagebrush habitat on the planet, but if it's only a hundred acres it won't be suitable for grouse.

Tanner said he is like most ranchers: they want to see sage-grouse on their lands. He recounted the experience of flushing grouse while driving cattle. He was intrigued to see one bird veer off and then realized a golden eagle was "herding" the bird apart from the flock. Another eagle appeared and dove for the bird, making a direct hit. It was a scene that depicted the eons-old story of predator versus prey. "The eagles were working together," he said. "Seeing things like that tells me I'm doing something right, attracting all sorts of wildlife to the land. Living conditions may seem harsh here, but it is where we like to live."

To answer Carson's implicit question: the Sagebrush Sea should be preserved in order to maintain the many species that depend on it, including humans. The interests of ranchers like Tanner and scientists like Hagen overlap in a single iconic species: the sage-grouse.

The bird is at the center of a storm over land use in the Sagebrush Sea. Diminished habitat due to human development threatens its survival. The U.S. Fish and Wildlife Service, after much public debate, in September 2015 declined to place greater sage-grouse on the Endangered Species List. Instead, a massive, multistate conservation movement called the Sage Grouse Initiative has brought together ranchers, environmentalists, corporations, universities, and government agencies to work cooperatively to benefit the bird and its habitat. Hagen is upbeat about the outlook for sage-grouse. "Once sagebrush has begun to be reestablished, sage-grouse seize the opportunity and begin to return," Hagen said. "Three or four years after the 2012 Holloway Fire, populations started to recover. The vagaries of climate can take a toll on nesting success even in the best conditions, but on the whole I am very optimistic we can turn the tide."

The expanse of the Sagebrush Sea, the last great dark place, continues to be fragmented, abused, and exploited. Once vast, its quality and quantity are diminishing as fast as the sage-grouse flocks that once darkened the sky. But it is all the birds have; they live here and nowhere else. It is where their story begins.

Sage-grouse researcher Christian Hagen measures the composition and structure of a plant community to understand how sage-grouse might use the habitat after junipers have been removed.

Lightning strikes can cause fires that help renew native grasses and forbs. But at drier, lower-elevation sites where cheatgrass grows (left), wildfires spread rapidly and destroy the slow-growing sagebrush. Lack of fires at higher elevation can create conditions for juniper to invade sagebrush habitat (above).

Vast areas of cheatgrass crowd out native sagebrush, leaving little habitat for sage-grouse. Cheatgrass is an exotic plant unintentionally introduced to Western landscapes around 1910. When fire destroys native vegetation like sagebrush, cheatgrass often takes over.

Desi Coombs, 12, gets her horse ready at 4:30 a.m. for the annual cattle branding on a ranch in Nevada. Desi has grown up with the concept of conserving wildlife while making a living on the land.

The Great Basin was created over thousands of years when huge blocks of the earth's crust were uplifted, then eroded over time to create cliffs and other visually stunning rock formations.

The Great Basin is one of the last dark places
on Earth. More than 200,000 square miles
of the Sagebrush Sea are here, creating
the vistas that Westerners hold dear.

Sage-grouse depend on sagebrush for everything: nesting cover, camouflage for young chicks, and the nutrient-rich forage they need to survive. The birds have elongated gizzards and toes that can dig through snow, adaptations that allow them to survive on sagebrush.

Sagebrush can survive and thrive in the harsh conditions meted out by the High Desert, from brutal cold to scorching heat. Without human disturbance, sagebrush plants can live 200 years or more.

Lupines bloom in the early summer in the
High Desert. Many varieties of wildflowers
and forbs decorate the landscape,
attracting pollinators and other insects
that grouse and other wildlife depend on.

In addition to sagebrush, sage-grouse eat a variety of insects and forbs abundant in the Sagebrush Sea.

Within the seemingly empty Sagebrush Sea live countless species of wildlife, including (clockwise) golden eagle, pronghorn, rough-legged hawk and Brewer's sparrow. They find shelter and sustenance among the many species of sagebrush and other plants that make up their habitat.

FOLLOWING PAGE

Once vast, the Sagebrush Sea, the last great dark place, is disappearing fast. But it is all the birds have; they live here and nowhere else.

Native Americans lived in harmony with this landscape and the wildlife it nurtured, including sage-grouse. They relied on them to nourish themselves physically and spiritually.

Levon Big Knife, a Chippewa-Cree and Shoshone, has been performing the "chicken dance" for more than a decade. According to legend, the power to dance like sage-grouse was bestowed on a young man by his spirit-helper after he watched sage-grouse strut. The dance celebrates grouse and Native Americans' relationship with the bird. Big Knife is a third-generation chicken dancer.

Pictographs like this one found in central Oregon tell the ancient story of human and wildlife interaction. Native Americans depended on animals for their physical and spiritual wellbeing. Their stories live on through legends and lore passed from generation to generation.

Sage-Grouse Legends of the Wasco and Northern Paiute

Wilson Wewa, Spiritual Leader, Columbia River Plateau

I have been collecting oral histories of my people all my life. I am half Northern Paiute and half Nez Perce, but these legends come from the Wasco people who lived along the Columbia River near The Dalles, in Oregon. The Confederated Tribes of Warm Springs are made up of Wasco and Walla Walla tribes that were forced onto a reservation in Warm Springs, Oregon, in 1855. In 1882 the Northern Paiute were moved onto the central Oregon reservation, which completed the confederacy.

The stories reflect the reverence my people feel for sage-grouse and all of nature. Without nature, we humans cannot exist. It saddens me to see the changes in the world today—habitat destruction, global warming, the stealing away of our clean water and air. People have lost their reverence for nature—they take it for granted that there will always be the earth beneath us, food to eat, and water to drink. I hope people will learn from nature: what happened to the passenger pigeon, what happened to Native Americans—that can happen again if we don't learn to care for all living things.

Here is one of the stories my people used to tell:

A long time ago, there was a lady who lost her husband. In her grief she wandered out into the desert and was crying in her sorrow. Then she heard noises like singing, so she went to investigate, and it was the noises from the sage-grouse. They were singing and dancing. The sage-grouse leader knew that she was in sorrow and talked to her and told her that she can't remain in sorrow all the time and that it would make her sick. He told her, "I'll give you this song and the dance," and so they incorporated that dance among the Wasco people. It became a dance of renewal of life, a dance of joy.

There are other tribes, too, that have stories about the sage-grouse. The Northern Paiute people have a similar story:

The hunters had gone out to hunt the deer and the antelope. When they were out in the desert, they heard that popping kind of noise. They wondered what made that noise, and when they came over the hill, it was the sage-grouse "facing off" to one another. So from the sage-grouse the Paiute people learned how to make war on other tribes. Sometimes when you come together like that, the birds will go back apart from one another, and they might walk off from one another. That would be a peaceful way, but there are times when they actually crash into one another with their wings and hit one another, and that's when they war.

In those days, there were lots of sage hens compared with now. In Central Oregon, all that area was pretty much just nothing but sagebrush. In a way, the sage-grouse are like us Indians—they're getting pushed to little pieces of land in order to survive. Stories like these keep them alive in our memory.

The Spectacular Dance

A male sage-grouse is in full breeding regalia in southern Idaho.

Males begin to gather before dawn on a lek in southern Wyoming. Males congregate weeks before females appear. Sage-grouse are birds of habit, gathering on the same leks year after year for generations.

THE SAGEBRUSH SEA IS DOTTED WITH STAGES WHERE sage-grouse perform one of the most flamboyant mating displays in nature: the swish, pop, whistling sounds; the spiked tail, magnificent ruff, and inflated yellow-green air sacs. Lacking decoration or lights, their stages (leks) are mostly large, sparsely vegetated areas that are used each year for the birds' spectacular dance. Males gather here beginning in late winter to early spring as their ancestors have done for thousands of years.

The male sage-grouse arrive each morning before daybreak to stake out the best territories for the upcoming show. They fight, preen, and strut among themselves until the females put in an appearance a month or more later. The center of the lek is the most coveted, and birds fight for dominance and for the preferred territories. Older birds seek center stage, driving young upstarts to the fringes. An individual male's territory may be as small as six square yards, if it is near the center of the lek, or a hundred square yards near the periphery.

The older birds have passed previous years' initiations and do not cede their territories easily. Fights break out. The birds parry, feint, and charge each other with wing, beak, and claw to secure the best sites, which are won often by older birds but always by stronger birds. The "master cock" with the best territory will breed with a majority of the females, consigning his younger, weaker rivals to the possibility of not breeding at all.

Even before daybreak, the males begin their dance. Their white breast feathers glow in the half-light. The grouse rapidly inflate and deflate their two bright, bare-skin vocal sacs, creating eerie spots across the landscape and producing ghostly popping noises as the sacs (esophageal pouches) resonate the passage of air.

When the sun illuminates the dance floor, the full spectacle of the performance is revealed. The males are in full breeding regalia, sporting fluffy white ruffs that sweep down their breasts. The ruffs are composed of white feathers with strong, downward- and backward-pointing tips, so that when a male rubs his wings against them, they make a loud whooshing sound. Decorative dangling head feathers (filoplumes) crown each side of his head. His sharply pointed tail feathers fan out behind him like a shield. Bright yellow patches over his eyes accentuate his costume, but it is the brilliant flashing air sacs that dominate the spectacle.

The male begins the dance by sweeping his wings across his chest with a swishing noise and an upward jerk of his head as his air sacs quickly protrude from his chest like bulbous yellow-green eggs. He bounces, deflating his air sacs with a series of loud popping noises. After a slight pause, there is another wing swish and a head jerk, followed by a brief glimpse of the air sacs. He makes three low-pitched hoots followed by a hollow plopping sound as the sacs deflate. He repeats this performance continuously, up to ten times a minute all morning long.

The stage acoustics are spectacular, as well. The vast open spaces seem to fill with the burbling, hooting, popping sounds of the dance. In the still air, before the wind picks up, the otherworldly dance music dominates the landscape.

A male sage-grouse in full breeding regalia begins his strut with a wing swish and an upward jerk of his head as his air sacs inflate.

Let the Mating Begin

Females don't arrive on the lek until weeks after the males. Because they will go directly to nesting spots after breeding, weather dictates their timing. They may seem uninterested early in the mating season as they forage and peck, but like singles at a bar, they are checking out the scene. Their presence stimulates the males to guard their territories aggressively. Young males spar with one another at the edges of the lek and encroach on their elders to gain a higher-status territory near the center. The pace of the courtship dance picks up as males vie for the females' attention. Occasionally, however, the performance is interrupted by the unwelcome arrival of a predator, and all the birds leave the lek for the cover of sagebrush.

As the season progresses, females become more interested in what the males have to offer. When ready, a female will crouch low, inviting the dominant male to breed with her. One or two dominant males will breed with all the females; the other males are mere understudies to the few stars' performances. Hens congregate around the dominant males. Some biologists have speculated this is "copying" behavior—they congregate around a male because other hens have already judged him to possess superior genes, based on his dominance on the lek and the vigor of his dance. The younger, less successful males may try to attract a hen's attention by appearing to be successful, hovering near groups of females and even assuming a mating posture. One was even observed attempting to mate with a cow pie, either in order to convince the females of his prowess or out of sheer frustration.

Females compete as well, jockeying to be first in line for mating with the "master cock" and often knocking another contender out of the way or even alighting on another female's back as the male attempts to breed with her. As soon as a female has been bred, she will leave the lek and head for nesting territory with good sagebrush cover, usually about three or four miles from the lek. Older, experienced females may have already selected a nest site, but younger hens are likely to seek a site after breeding.

Lekking comes to an end when all the hens have been bred, usually in May. The males will stop displaying their brilliant breeding regalia and congregate together in flocks, their fierce competition forgotten. They will have no role in nesting or caring for the next generation.

The pace of the courtship dance picks up as males vie for the females' attention.

Why Birds Dance

The technical term for the sage-grouse's mating system (and that of many other species) is "lek polygyny." "Polygyny" denotes one male mating with many females and each female typically mating with only one male, usually with the females taking more or even sole responsibility for rearing the next generation of young. Lek polygyny is polygyny at its most extreme—with males gathering together to display for choosy females, attempting to mate as often as possible, and providing no resources or parental care. So why is it the male that dances and the female that chooses?

Evolution favors behaviors in females and males that lead to leaving a maximum number of offspring, but the behaviors that benefit one sex do not always benefit the other. Because females have such a great investment in mating—they will raise only a few clutches of eggs during their lifetimes—they typically benefit from choosing a high-quality sperm source rather than seeking to mate with many males. Males, in contrast, produce lots of sperm and therefore benefit from seeking to copulate with as many mates as possible. The grand stages of the Sagebrush Sea allow males to demonstrate their

suitability for mating by fighting off competitors and engaging in physically demanding dance displays. Females are the critics in the audience, judging which of the males they will accept to father their offspring.

Many factors play a role in how species' mating systems evolve: life history, ecology, and the distribution of resources. If both sexes are needed to ensure survival of the young, then a male gains no benefit by seeking multiple females because none of his offspring would survive if he abandons them. Females of the species would be choosing a male on the basis of his potential for providing resources and parental care, not just sex appeal. Leks tend to be found in systems where food is widely distributed, so that males cannot monopolize it by making a territory around it to exclude other males and females who refuse to mate with him. For sage-grouse, food is widespread and abundant, and females are able to successfully care for their young without help from males. Because they can raise young on their own, female sage-grouse may have more to gain by being picky about the sires of their young—who will pass down their genes for sexiness and good health to their offspring—than by finding males who will co-parent with them.

The term for the stage—lek—was coined in the 1860s by the naturalist Llewelyn Lloyd in his book *The Game Birds and Wild Fowl of Sweden and Norway* to describe the area where black grouse seemed to "play." A diversity of species of animals—including fish, insects, some mammals and amphibians, and many bird species—have independently evolved lekking behavior. But it is a rare mating system—about 90 percent of birds are monogamous and raise the young together (though they are known to cheat on one another!), and fewer than 1 percent of birds form leks. Within this tiny fraction, many of the most flamboyant specimens on the avian family tree are found, such as peacocks, bustards, birds of paradise, manakins, bowerbirds, and of course, sage-grouse and their relatives.

Sage-grouse use the same leks year after year; if the bird population grows, a satellite lek may appear nearby. If a lek is destroyed, the males will try to strut on suitable ground near it. Many leks have been in use for hundreds of years. Strutting grounds are relatively flat and barren of trees or other predator

The sage-grouse perform one of the most flamboyant mating displays in nature. They use the same stages every year for their spectacular dance, just as their ancestors have done for thousands of years.

perches, and they may range from less than an acre to almost a hundred acres in size. Several dozen males may use a lek, though some leks attract many more. In earlier days, when their populations were much larger, up to eight hundred males were documented on single leks.

Wildlife biologists from eleven states in sage-grouse range use lek counts each spring to keep tabs on sage-grouse populations. The Western Association of Fish and Wildlife Agencies reported that in 2015, 85,674 males were counted on 3,559 leks and extrapolated the lek counts to estimate a rangewide population of about 400,000 birds.

Survival of the Sexiest

The sage-grouse dance is one of the most flamboyant mating displays in nature: the swish, pop, whistling sounds; the spiked tail, magnificent ruff, and inflated yellow-green air sacs. Yet an entire performance may have to be canceled if one of the birds' many predators—a golden eagle or ferruginous hawk, for example—appears for the show. Would a drabber bird with a more subdued mating ritual be less likely to attract predators, to survive longer?

Charles Darwin pondered questions like this when he wrote *The Origin of Species,* published in 1859. That groundbreaking book outlined the tenets of natural selection, describing how traits that help an individual survive and reproduce in its environment will be passed on to the next generation, while traits that inhibit survival and reproduction will eventually disappear from populations. But what about a male bird with a large, elaborate train—a peacock, for example, with many shining feather "eyes"? Certainly the gaudy plumage has questionable value for the bird's survival and may, in fact, hinder a fast escape from a predator. As he worked on his theory, Darwin noted humorously in a letter to a colleague, "The sight of a feather in a peacock's tail makes me sick."

But eventually Darwin worked out the concept of sexual selection, a corollary of natural selection. The answer lies, in large part, in the larger tail's power to attract more peahens than do the males' tails that are smaller. With more mating opportunities, a male with genes for a large tail tends to generate more offspring than those with smaller tails. Sexual selection, which can explain the brilliant colors, elaborate mating dances, and loud courtship calls, might facetiously be called not "survival of the fittest" but "survival of the sexiest." To pass along one's genes, one must both survive *and* reproduce. In the

case of sage-grouse, there is no evidence that females prefer brighter, bigger air sacs or longer tail feathers, but the research of Robert Gibson of the University of Nebraska and Jack Bradbury of Cornell University has indicated that the vigor and energy of the dance (as measured by the strut rate) determine which males are successful. Similarly, Gail Patricelli, a professor of evolution and ecology at the University of California, Davis, and her graduate students have found that females select males that dance with the most vigor and the best sounds. They once observed a male mate with females twenty-three times in as many minutes. Throughout that morning, he mated with thirty-six females; in one breeding season, he mated 157 times.

"It seemed from observation that this sage-grouse had more energy, health, and vigor than his rivals. He was just in complete domination of the other males on the lek," said Patricelli. "He may have had a whole suite of good genes that would be beneficial to pass on to offspring, and females may select him for that reason. But just plain sexiness may have had a lot to do with it, too."

Fembots That Fool the Eye

Patricelli built her first robot bird to resemble a female satin bowerbird, a lekking species native to Australia with remarkable courtship behaviors, but

Leks are large areas devoid of trees and shrubs that could serve as perches for predators.

any particular species she studies provides insights into her deeper questions; she wants to understand the social interactions between males and females and the factors that determine how females select breeding partners. Therefore she was intrigued to learn at a conference that the sound made by sage-grouse air sacs emanates from the sides of the chest, not the front or the beak. This may explain why males often stand sideways to the females with which they wish to mate. Their distinctive traits and elaborate mating dance persuaded her to make sage-grouse her new focus of study.

She decided that building a dummy sage hen that she could control remotely would help her understand the complex mating rituals she witnessed on the lek. Her first sage-grouse "fembot," developed in 2007, was a primitive device (named "Anna Nicole") that could only move on G-scale model-train tracks. Fembots of the current generation (named "Snooki," "Salt," and "Pepa") move on all-terrain spiked wheels that rotate independently to be more maneuverable. Sophisticated electronics that include sound and video recorders reside within a resin cast made from a grouse-shaped taxidermy body form that is covered with a grouse skin. The fembots can be controlled from long distances with a model-airplane remote control. The results are amazingly realistic; they can peck, stretch, tilt, and turn. Grass conceals the wheels. Even the males are fooled. "It's hard to tell the difference between a real female and a fembot," said Patricelli. "And males aren't picky, which makes it easier. They're highly motivated to mate."

The technology allows Patricelli and her research team to study the mating behaviors of male and female sage-grouse. They determined, for example, that successful males slow their display rate when females are distant and speed it up when they come closer, allowing them to increase their endurance by moderating their energy output and still stimulate females by increasing the quality and quantity of their dance.

Observations like this result in greater understanding of animal behavior and the factors that play a role in sexual selection. "We are learning the traits that females choose, which will then be passed on to offspring," Patricelli said. "Traits can evolve to be more elaborate just because females favor them."

No Home on the Range

Patricelli is applying her basic research on mating signals to conservation purposes by studying the effect of noise on lekking sage-grouse. "There are many practical applications to what we're learning about sage-grouse behavior," she said. "Declining sage-grouse populations are a huge concern, so factors that affect their ability to reproduce are of great interest."

Core sage-grouse areas have been identified in some states, allowing populations to be protected by reducing habitat changes brought, for example, by the oil and gas extraction operations that are proliferating throughout the Sagebrush Sea. State and federal agencies have adopted policies that limit sage-grouse disruption in core areas.

In the case of sage-grouse, research hasn't determined whether females prefer brighter, bigger air sacs or longer tail feathers, but it has indicated that the vigor and energy of the dance (as measured by the strut rate) determine which males are successful.

Patricelli and her students have learned that the birds are very sensitive to noise, enough to cause significant declines in attendance on leks. Most of the research has been conducted near Lander, Wyoming, in the Wind River Range, and the Pinedale Anticline, which is an area of massive energy development. "The sagebrush steppe is a naturally quiet place, especially early in the morning when lek activity begins and before the wind picks up," said Patricelli. "My colleague Skip Ambrose has found that the average noise level is seven to fifteen decibels. That's quieter than many humans have experienced." She and her research colleagues are finding that lekking is disrupted when noise reaches about twenty-five decibels.

Noise rules have been tightened in response to Patricelli's research, but she said it's not enough.

You can just imagine how the noise of a drilling rig, for example, dominates the soundscape for the birds when there's almost no other noise out there. It's like that loud ticking of a clock in the middle of the night when you can't sleep—except much, much louder. Limiting development near leks and surrounding nesting areas would be the most significant changes [for sage-grouse conservation], as well as limiting vehicle traffic. Naturally, there is resistance to doing this.

Lekking habitat is under siege from changes to the Sagebrush Sea, both man-made, from roads, utilities, fences, and development, and human-induced, such as fire and invasive species. Sage-grouse, which have strutted for millennia on the same grounds, are finicky about changes. They do not adapt well to loss of their native lands. Appreciation for the bird is growing, however, in large part due to their spectacular dance on stages bereft of sounds and lights. The dance perpetuates the species by leading to the next generation of sage-grouse, and it may also perpetuate grouse populations by leading humans to care enough to conserve them.

The strutting males do not wait for spring to begin
their ritual dance. This male braves Wyoming's snow
and ice to begin the performance in February.

Males stake out territories on the lek, sparring with others over the most coveted areas near the center. Territories may vary from a few square yards near the center to much more expansive sizes along the periphery. The size of the bird, its stamina, territory on the lek, and the vigor of the strut all play a role in establishing male dominance.

FOLLOWING PAGE

A male sage-grouse and his breath appear to glow as the morning sun lights the stage where he performs his mating dance.

In a sequence of moves that lasts just two seconds, males begin their strut standing straight, wings at side.

The white neck feathers raise slightly, exposing the air sacs. The bird rapidly moves his wings against his breast feathers, producing a swishing sound accompanied by a low growl, presumably also produced by the feathers.

The olive-colored air sacs inflate again, and the bird emits a quick series of three low-pitched hooting noises, followed by a hollow plopping sound as the air sacs deflate. This is immediately followed by a sharp whistle and another extremely rapid sac inflation and deflation plop.

Each stage of the bizarre performance lasts just fractions of a second, and the entire performance can be repeated as much as ten times a minute.

Decorative head feathers, called filoplumes, add a distinctive crowning touch to the bird's white fur-like collar. The sharply pointed tail feathers (far right) and white-tipped under-tail coverts make a formidable frame for the bird's big body, which can weigh more than seven pounds.

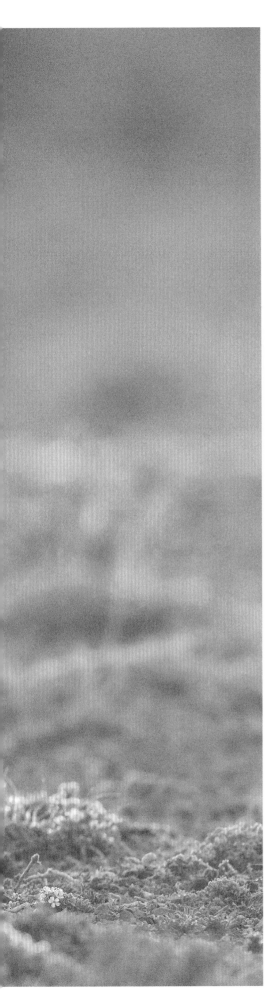

Mating is a game of dominance among male sage-grouse.
Sage-grouse fight fiercely over territories on the lek. These males
(left) are locked in a standoff. The stand-off may progress to
aggressive fighting, but birds are rarely injured in the process.

Male sage-grouse vie with beak and claw for prime territory on the lek. The winner gets not only the best area, but the chance to breed most of the females. One or two dominant males breed more than half the females. Sub-dominant males continue to strut, but their chances of mating are slim.

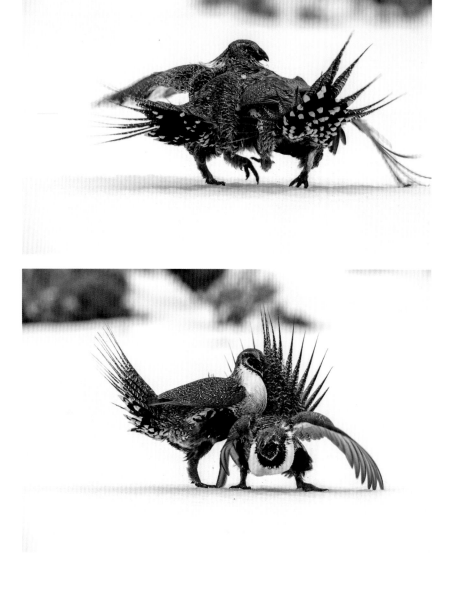

Females arrive weeks after the males appear on the lek. At first they may seem uninterested, but they are browsing in order to select the most dominant male with which to breed. Their presence stimulates the males to dance more vigorously and to fight for their territories more aggressively.

FOLOWING PAGE

Females congregate around the dominant male and will sometimes fight among themselves for proximity to him. Some biologists believe young hens copy the behavior of other females rather than individually selecting the dominant male based on his attributes.

When ready to mate, a female lowers
her body with outstretched wings,
inviting the attentions of the male.

After the elaborate courtship display by the male, breeding itself is straightforward. The female indicates her readiness to mate by crouching with outspread wings; the male approaches and mounts her; the female shakes herself and departs. The entire process can be over in less than ten seconds.

A young male mounts a cow-pie. This unusual behavior may reflect inexperience, frustration, copying behavior, or an attempt to attract female birds.

A young male is chased from the territory of a more dominant bird. Older birds seek center stage, driving young and inexperienced ones to the fringes.

The golden eagle is one of many predators that often prey on sage-grouse. The mating display is dangerous business without the benefit of cover.

Sagebrush is the birds' primary source of food and is also essential for nesting and cover from predators. All the birds on a lek will flee to areas that provide sagebrush cover if a predator approaches.

The sage-grouse mating instinct is strong.
Males begin congregating early in the year
when winter has a firm grip on the landscape
and continue the ritual even when cold, driving
rain creates harsh conditions (above).

Lekking activities come to an end when all the females have been bred, usually in May. Males will stop displaying and leave the lek for summer habitat. They will have no role in nesting or caring for the next generation.

A remote-controlled robot disguised as a female sage-grouse—a fembot—approaches a male sage-grouse as biologist Gail Patricelli and her colleague, Alan Krakauer (right), study breeding behavior from a blind near the lek.

Before It's Too Late

Gail Patricelli, University of California, Davis

I'm not a morning person, so getting out of my warm sleeping bag at four in the morning during the spring sage-grouse lekking season requires all the willpower I can muster. But after some coffee and a granola bar, after climbing into the same muddy field clothes and boots I've worn all season, after exiting the warm field trailer into the bracing cold, after loading up the gear in the truck, after scraping ice off the windshield, after pulling out of the driveway through crunching snow or frozen mud, after ambling in the truck over rutted two-track dirt roads through the sagebrush, after carrying the gear to my hunting blind by headlamp, after popping up the blind and crawling inside, after readying my cameras and audio recording equipment, and after turning off my headlamp to listen quietly … then I am finally rewarded with the best part of the day—the arrival of the first sage-grouse to the lek—which unfolds in the darkness as a story in sounds.

I fell in love with sage-grouse as a graduate student, when I attended a talk by Marc Dantzker at a scientific conference. (Marc later became a collaborator.) Marc talked about the bizarre and mysterious sounds of the sage-grouse strut. These sounds resonate and radiate from the vocal sacs on the males' chests and sound more like a frog than a bird. The sounds beam outward from the bird at odd angles, quietest directly in front of the body and loudest to the left and right, in front of the two vocal sacs, and even behind the bird. Male sage-grouse displaying for females often rotate between struts, facing off toward the distance or turning their backs on females. These odd angles make it appear as if the males were ignoring the females, but in fact they are beaming their sounds directly at females at maximum volume.

I was thrilled to learn about this quirk of sage-grouse vocal physiology and behavior because I was interested in understanding how Darwin's process of sexual selection by female choice can favor the evolution not just of showy traits like the sage-grouse strut and the peacock's train but also of what we might call social skills—the ability to interact appropriately with the opposite sex—by observing and responding to the social conditions of courtship. Sage-grouse are perfect for studying this process because males need to reposition themselves constantly to track moving females with their sounds. They also need to respond to competing males and the behaviors of females in the bustling marketplace of the lek.

The sage-grouse have kept my team and me busy for a dozen years so far, and we don't plan to stop anytime soon. This basic research on sage-grouse breeding behaviors by my team and by other researchers beginning decades before me has taught us a great deal about questions larger than sage-grouse, such as how sexual selection works and how leks evolve. This work has also taught us details about sage-grouse biology that are critical for conservation of this species and its habitat, such as the degree to which noise pollution impacts sage-grouse breeding and how to reduce those impacts.

We've found that sage-grouse are picky, sensitive birds, so well adapted to the extraordinary silence of calm mornings on the sagebrush steppe that they are disturbed by even low levels of noise pollution. They are exquisitely adapted to the harsh landscape in which they live, but they are very poorly adapted to human presence in that landscape. That is why I and many other biologists have spent decades working with the goal of trying to understand and protect this North American icon before it's too late. When the alarm clock goes off at four o'clock, that goal and my curiosity about these fascinating animals help me haul myself out of my warm sleeping bag for yet another morning on the lek.

The
Perilous Life

A newly hatched sage-grouse chick rests under
sagebrush before beginning to explore the world.

Clouds bearing snow approach the Great Basin
in southern Oregon, where average precipitation
is between nine and twelve inches per year.

AFTER BEING COURTED IN ONE OF THE MOST SPECTACULAR displays in nature, female grouse leave the lek as soon as they are bred. They may travel ten or more miles from the lek to select a nesting site. Adult females have usually scouted and selected nesting areas before mating, but inexperienced young females start the process with little more than instinct before laying eggs and raising a brood.

The hen seeks low, heavy clumps of sagebrush or cool-season bunchgrasses to conceal her nest, with a watering source nearby. A variety of forbs will provide an insect base for the young chicks. More than 90 percent of nests are located under sagebrush, many of them well concealed by thick growth. The hen may return to within a few hundred yards of the same nesting territory each year if the habitat remains suitable.

She constructs the nest in a shallow depression eight to ten inches in diameter and lines it with feathers. About four days after breeding she begins to lay six to ten oval, buff-green eggs with brown speckles at a rate of somewhat less than one egg per day (averaging about three days for every two eggs). She periodically turns the eggs to prevent the developing yolk from sticking to the inside of the shell. Eggs begin to hatch twenty-four to twenty-seven days after being laid. Since male grouse play no role in nesting or rearing of the young birds, the hen must forage on her own, leaving vulnerable eggs unattended while she feeds rapidly on insects, sage, and forbs.

Nesting is a dangerous business, with badgers, ravens, and other predators looking for a tasty and nutritious egg or chick to snack on. Nesting success has been studied in more than ten states. The results have varied widely, but on average only half of all nests produce one or more chicks. Higher rates occur in areas of ideal nesting habitat—rich in sage, thick grasses, other forbs, and low shrubs—and lower rates in areas where habitat has been altered through intensive grazing, herbicide spraying, plowing, or burning.

If a hen's eggs are destroyed while she is still laying, she may use reserves of viable sperm from her most recent breeding to lay a second clutch of eggs. If her eggs are destroyed while she is incubating them, she may return to the lek for a second mating. Most hens will attempt to lay a second clutch if the nest is predated at an early stage, but the longer they sit on the nest the less likely they are to attempt another. Males stay on the lek, continuing their mating dance, for a full month after most females have left. If the chicks are killed, the hen will likely put her reserves of energy into surviving the winter rather than renesting. Because sage-grouse are long-lived compared with pheasant or quail, high reproductive success over a lifetime is more important than success in a single year. A hen may have four to six more years of nesting attempts ahead of her.

Upon hatching, sage-grouse chicks are covered with fluffy feathers, their natal down. The down is grayish, strikingly marked with patches of brown and black on the body, wings, and head. Newly hatched chicks weigh about twenty-seven grams, less than an ounce, just a bit more than five nickels. These young are precocial—within a few hours after hatching, they are dry, active, and ready to leave the nest. The nest is abandoned soon after all the eggs have hatched, and the hen does not seek another nesting site but beds down under cover with her chicks under or around her. A researcher in 1950 observed a hen on her nest at ten in the morning with four chicks and three eggs. By seven in the evening of that day the hen and seven chicks had traveled two hours to a wet meadow that was 162 yards from the nest.

Survival over the next few months is fraught with danger. Biologists estimate that at least half of all chicks hatched in the spring will perish before winter. A Utah study concluded that there need to be 2.25 juveniles to each hen to keep populations stable.

Chick Mortality

There are basically three ways to study sage-grouse chick mortality, said wildlife biologist Phillip Street, a PhD candidate at the University of Nevada, Reno, but only one of them doesn't risk having a bad outcome for the chicks.

Attaching a transmitter to the chick's back requires lots of handling and disrupts the brood. Another method, called a "flush count," requires that the

Female grouse leave the lek as soon as they are bred. Nesting sites are usually two to ten miles from the lek. They require a nearby water source and sagebrush to conceal the nest.

A typical nest contains six to ten oval, buff-green eggs speckled with brown. Just an hour out of the egg, a sage-grouse chick embarks on a life fraught with danger.

hen have a radio transmitter; flushing her away from the brood in the very early morning allows the chicks to be counted. The trouble with this method, said Street, is that when the hen leaves the chicks, they are subjected to the cold and more vulnerable to predators. Street relies on a third method designed to have less impact on the hen and chicks. He sets up a camera and tripod near a radio-tagged hen very early in the morning when the chicks are nestled around or under her. When it is warm enough for the chicks to survive without the hen's body heat, they will come out to forage. The hen stays close by and keeps watch for predators. If a predator comes close, she will make a distressed display to draw the predator away from the chicks.

Street has studied chick mortality since 2013 in order to help determine how grazing affects sage-grouse populations. He has learned so far that hens that move their chicks to higher elevations or wet meadows have a better chance of brood success than those that do not. "The birds hatch in June, when the Nevada desert is drying out," he said. "The birds may be only two to three days old when they move to better conditions in search of protein-rich forbs. They won't survive if they don't move."

Timing plays a big role in nesting success, too, according to Street. The chicks of hens that nest early have lower survival rates because they are more susceptible to cold weather and inadequate cover, but if they survive their early weeks of life, they have more time to grow before having to move to areas with more moisture. Chicks should be mostly grown by the end of summer in order to survive the winter. Hens that nest late may have more favorable conditions initially, but they risk the onset of hot, dry weather and their chicks have less time to grow before the landscape dries out. "It's a balancing act that varies from year to year depending on the weather and greenup," he said.

Hens and their broods that successfully reach higher elevations or wet meadows still face a long list of dangers. Predators are drawn to these areas, too, and will feast on defenseless sage-grouse chicks. Street believes most predation is from other birds, but a host of mammals—coyotes, badgers, weasels, bobcats, and panthers—prey on the young birds. And then there is the issue of grazing.

Open Range and Grazing

Wet meadows that draw grouse and other wildlife also attract cattle and feral horses. Sometimes ranchers build ponds to hold water for their cattle. When the vegetation is removed by grazing or trampling, the soil erodes and the water table is lowered, making it unreachable to typical meadow vegetation. Cattle and horses also eat and trample sagebrush, the mainstay of the grouse's diet.

"Feral horses are a big deal out here," said Street. In 2013 and 2014, more than a thousand feral horses were removed from the Sheldon National Wildlife Refuge in northern Nevada. Livestock had been removed from the refuge ten years earlier. The absence of grazing animals gives wildlife researchers the opportunity to study their impact on sage-grouse populations. The results of the study won't be known for several years, but the number of collaborating funders—the U.S. Fish and Wildlife Service, the Bureau of Land Management, the state of Nevada, and several nonprofit organizations—indicates the degree of interest in maintaining sage-grouse survival, Street said.

His focus is on the effect of feral horses and livestock grazing on sagebrush habitat in prime nesting and brood-rearing areas. Some ranchers in sage-grouse territory are taking steps to avoid damage from grazing cattle. Jay Tanner, owner of the Grouse Creek Ranch in the Great Basin, and his neighbors have agreed to keep their cattle on more marginal land during the crucial months when hens and chicks need the abundant insects and native grasses for food and cover that are found in wet areas. "They tell us that these riparian areas are as biologically diverse as the rain forest," he said. "They're just narrow strips of moisture that attract all manner of wildlife." In late summer, when calves are getting to the weaning stage, the ranchers move the cows from the dry, marginal land to the wetter meadows. By then, the sage hens and their chicks have flown to higher elevations seeking sagebrush.

The Bureau of Land Management owns about 80 percent of the sage-grouse habitat in the basin, but about 80 percent of the prime brood-rearing areas are on private land. "Some people would like to remove cattle from public lands, but if you take livestock off those marginal lands it will ultimately damage sage-grouse populations because it would force us to use those important riparian areas that we own," Tanner said. "As ranchers, we know we need to work together with federal land managers. We have a good relationship, and we work hard to keep it that way."

In many other areas of sage-grouse territory, however, wet meadows, particularly near urban areas or oil and gas drilling, are highly coveted for development potential. Sage-grouse populations, once counted in the millions, have declined precipitously as prime habitat for nesting and rearing chicks has diminished.

Juvenile Grouse

Young grouse must grow fast in order to face harsh winters in sagebrush country. They are ready to make short flights within two weeks of hatching. In one study, conducted in Wyoming in the 1950s, five- and six-week-old birds were able to fly 163 yards about 30 feet off the ground, clocking in at up to thirty miles per hour. By mid-August, the birds have attained full juvenile plumage, though the wing and tail feathers are not fully developed.

By late summer and early fall, young birds of both sexes show a triangular patch of feathers with dark spots and light vertical streaks on the upper breast. Young female birds will gradually lose this distinctive patch in favor of the all-over camouflage plumage and attain their mature size in the fall of their first year. By mid-October, immature males will begin to show the black throat and neck band that characterize their nuptial coloration. They may be a pound heavier than the females, but are still not as heavy as a mature male, which will weigh from four to seven pounds and measure twenty-two to almost thirty inches long. The greater sage-grouse is the largest of the grassland grouse species, and it is second only to wild turkey among gallinaceous birds in North America. Females will average only half the size of males. The size difference between male and female is greater in sage-grouse than in most other birds. By early December, two patches of white begin to show on the upper breasts of males, over their air sacs. This nuptial plumage continues to develop throughout the winter and will be fully present in time for breeding season.

Young birds are well adapted by camouflage and instinct to survive in their perilous surroundings. They respond to the mother's warning and alarm calls by dispersing in all directions to hiding places. When surprised by an intruder or predator, though, their immediate reaction is to squat down and remain motionless, permitting their camouflage to conceal them against the landscape. A mother bird will also attempt to lead an intruder away from the nest by feigning a wing injury and clumsily hopping on the ground. In some cases, she may also engage in battle by flying at an enemy hissing and cackling.

Late Summer and Early Fall

The chicks that survive the first few weeks of life must move quickly to a water source, particularly in their more arid ranges, where high temperatures and dry conditions spell danger for young birds. The hen moves them to a water

On average only half of all nests produce one or more chicks. Survival in the first few months of life is risky as well. At least half of all chicks hatched in the spring will perish before winter.

source, often at a higher elevation, where sagebrush and forbs provide food and protective cover.

As fall approaches, their diet gradually shifts to sagebrush, but they still need a water source, which is often shared with other high-desert wildlife—pronghorns, mule deer, ground squirrels, tiger salamanders, and a host of birds and predators—that will make a meal of a young sage-grouse if the opportunity arises.

Water is a rare commodity in much of the grouse's range. Areas with reliable water sources are often the first to be developed into ranches, communities, and urban and suburban sprawl. State populations throughout sage-grouse range have grown by almost one million people since the 1990s when declining sage-grouse numbers became a concern.

If young grouse can find a locale where they don't have to compete with pavement, cars, fences, buildings, and other human-made obstacles, their rapid growth helps prepare them for the harsh onset of winter. They may leave higher elevations near water sources to seek their prime requirement for survival, sagebrush. Sagebrush was once the most abundant shrub in North America, but changes to the landscape have limited its proliferation, often challenging the grouse's ability to find suitable winter habitat.

Fall Hunting Season and Populations

The sage-grouse is a sought-after trophy for many upland game hunters. Eight states—California, Colorado, Idaho, Montana, Nevada, Oregon, Utah, and Wyoming—have limited sage-grouse hunting seasons, mostly in September. Tom Christiansen is the sage-grouse program coordinator for the Wyoming Game and Fish Department. (Wyoming is home to about 38 percent of the overall sage-grouse population in North America.) He said for most popular game birds, such as pheasant and quail, hunting only removes "surplus" birds—about the same number that would likely die over the winter. But because sage-grouse have low winter mortality—sometimes even gaining weight during winter—fall hunting can be "additive," meaning it can have a greater effect on populations, which is why sage-grouse hunting seasons are conservative.

As the largest grouse in North America, sage-grouse is a sought-after trophy for many upland game hunters.

"The proportion of grouse that is taken by hunters is so small that it is inconsequential," Christiansen said. "Most hunters are usually the ones who want to regulate themselves because they have a vested interest. We don't have many hunters asking for more liberal seasons."

Hunters contribute to wildlife biologists' understanding of sage-grouse nesting success by providing a wing from birds that they kill, which reveals the age and sex of the bird. Wildlife biologists analyze the wings and arrive at estimates of the proportion of young birds in the population. The information gives a pretty accurate picture of whether there will be more or fewer birds counted on leks throughout their habitat the following spring. The 2016 results, said Christiansen, showed poor nesting success, but he cautioned that a single year does not make a trend; the previous two years had been good.

We are more concerned about long-term trends than annual variation. Sage-grouse populations tend to cycle, like rabbits. Some people call it population eruptions, when you have a couple of years of good production followed by a glide path down. The reason there's so much concern about sage-grouse is that the fifty-to-sixty-year trend is down. But if you look at it since the mid-1990s, when they were at their lowest, it has leveled off and in some cases gone up a bit.

Wyoming has been in the forefront of habitat protection because of the rapid development of oil and gas extraction there, but, Christiansen added, "In some areas, our impact on the landscape is too great. We've had some local population extirpations."

The edibility of sage-grouse is often called into question. When John Townsend wrote in 1834 that they were "so strong and bitter as not to be eatable," he was reflecting a common opinion about the bird's dietary reliance on sage leaves and the resulting strong flavor of their meat. Young birds are said to be milder in flavor, and many hunters insist that the meat is palatable as long as the bird is field-dressed immediately after being killed. For Christiansen, though, it's an acquired taste. He said, "If sage-grouse tasted like pheasant, they'd be extinct."

Roadblock on the Freeway of Life

In the fall, male sage-grouse congregate in flocks. They are slow to take flight, their heavy bodies more at home in the sage than the air. Once in flight, they can fly fast and far, but the first few hundred feet can be fraught with danger.

"For eons, grouse have been taking off and landing in huge flocks, early in the morning and late at night—low light, in other words," said Steve Chindgren, who hunts grouse with falcons near his home base of Eden, Wyoming. He is a widely recognized falconer and has studied sage-grouse since he was a child. His interest in falcons started early, too. "I saw a hawk, and it made me curious. I looked it up in the encyclopedia, and it made me hungry for more information." His curiosity led to a lifetime of research and observation of the sage-grouse. He has identified almost twenty sage-grouse leks previously unknown to the Wyoming Game and Fish Department, and he discovered a previously unrecognized threat to the birds: barbed-wire fences.

"I use a freeway analogy: take someone who drives the same freeway to work every morning for years. String a steel cable across the highway some morning and find out how many drivers see it." Chindgren counted sixty dead birds along a fence one morning as he conducted a grouse survey. He found a discarded soda pop can and hung it on the fence, making it more visible to the flying birds. That started him on a single-handed mission to mark as many miles of barbed-wire fence as he could. Local cafés and diners saved their pop cans for him. One day state game and fish agents conducting an aerial survey were mystified to see shiny objects stretching for miles along fencerows in all directions.

Tom Christiansen, the sage-grouse program coordinator for the Wyoming Game and Fish Department, conducted a study that showed 170 grouse fatalities due to fence collisions over two years in heavily used grouse areas. Use of reflective tape to mark fences led to a 70 percent reduction in accidents.

"Given all the technology available to us today, I can't understand why we rely on centuries-old means of controlling cattle. Bury a wire, put a chip in the cattle," said Chindgren, referring to the electronic fences common in suburban neighborhoods to control pets. "It's not as though building a four-foot-high fence with posts that rot over time saves money or labor, it's just that change occurs very slowly here."

Winter and Spring: The Cycle Renews

As temperatures drop and snow begins to fall, sage-grouse in the northern ranges can still flourish if both snow and sagebrush are abundant. Unlike deciduous plants, sagebrush remains green throughout the winter. Its leaves contain unusually high concentrations of protein needed by the birds to survive the winter.

The sage-grouse is unique among other gallinaceous birds for the structure of its digestive tract. Grain-eating birds need a thick, muscular gizzard to digest hard seeds and grains. Sage-grouse have evolved with their food source to digest the herbaceous sage leaves, so they don't need a strong gizzard or the grit that poultry need to digest hard seeds. Instead, they have an elongated gizzard that breaks down sage leaves. Eating snow helps grouse digest the pungent sage and furnishes the water they need to survive.

The birds have another evolutionary advantage to survive the ravages of winter: they develop small outgrowths on the sides of each of their three toes at the onset of cold weather. These comblike structures drop off in the spring, but during winter they function like snowshoes, allowing the birds to walk on top of the snow. Additionally, the inner side of the nail on the middle toe becomes enlarged, so the bird can also dig through snow to reach buried sagebrush leaves. The resulting excavations also provide a snug roosting place during harsh weather.

Sage-grouse depend on vast, open spaces of sagebrush for survival. Sagebrush provides the birds' primary source of food, nesting places, and shelter.

During winter, young male grouse develop their full breeding plumage. In February or early March, they begin to take their places on the lek along with other mature males, though their chances of mating with a female are slim. Females, including those hatched the previous spring, will arrive a month or two after the males. In May or early June, when females no longer appear on the lek, all the males—young and old—will leave the lek to seek good sagebrush habitat to renew their energy reserves after the mating season. The young females will take their chances with a clutch of eggs of their own for the first time, just as generations of sage-grouse have done before them. The cycle of life begins anew.

A sage-grouse hen stays close to her nest to guard it from predators. She may fluff out her feathers to appear larger and hiss, cackle, and fly at intruders to protect her vulnerable brood.

Concealed under heavy cover of sagebrush, a hen
will sit on her eggs for almost thirty days, taking
only short breaks to forage for food and water.

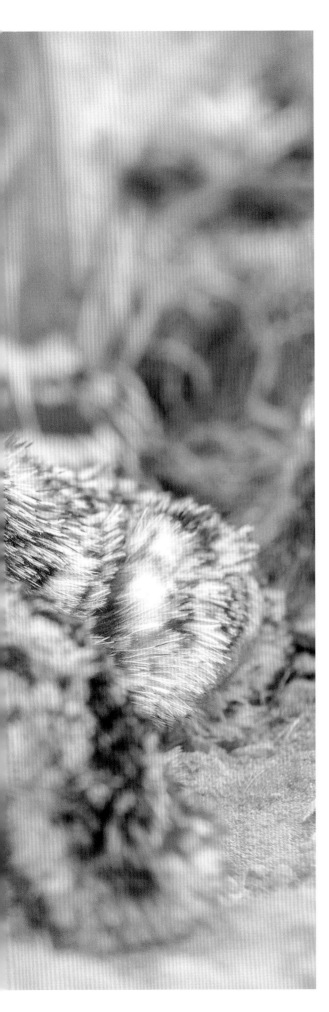

About four days after breeding, the hen lays six to ten oval, buff-green eggs. Eggs begin to hatch twenty-four to twenty-seven days after being laid.

Once hatched, sage-grouse chicks are covered with grayish fluffy feathers, marked with patches of brown and black on the body, wings, and head. Newly hatched, chicks weigh less than an ounce.

The hen will abandon her nest soon after chicks hatch, moving her brood to a secure habitat with food and water. These young chicks will stay together during the warm summer months.

Even at a young age, sage-grouse must travel long distances to find a water source during the dry summer. They are vulnerable to many predators during this time.

Sage-grouse chicks face many perils during their first months of life: roads, predators, and harsh conditions. At least half of all chicks hatched in the spring will perish before winter.

Chicks generally stay close to mom, but if a predator appears, she may attempt to lead it away from her chicks.

A chick that got left behind calls for the hen
before retreating into sagebrush cover.

FOLLOWING PAGE

A creek that runs through the High Desert in central
Wyoming reflects the setting of the summer sun.

In the High Desert, water is a precious commodity that attracts all kinds of life, including sage-grouse, predators, and livestock. Sometimes run-off from melting snow can create ephemeral lakes or "playas" that wildlife depend on, but they disappear quickly as the summer sun dries out the landscape.

Sage-grouse gather at a water source for an early morning drink, while keeping an eye out for ever-present danger.

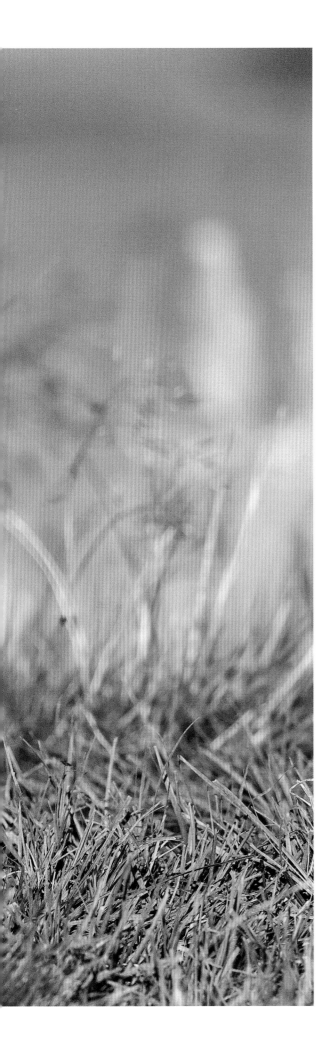

Males congregate during the summer and are often seen in large flocks. Mature male birds appear smaller without their elaborate breeding regalia, but they are still roughly twice as large as females.

Young birds stay together during the warm summer months for a better chance of survival. They are well adapted by camouflage and instinct to survive, but roughly half will die before winter.

Thick stands of rabbitbrush provide habitat for a host of species. Wildlife only lightly forage on this shrub, but it provides good cover for many nesting birds.

Female grouse feed heavily during the fall in preparation for the cold winter. They will soon move to their wintering ground at a higher elevation.

Sage-grouse chicks grow rapidly. By fall, they
reach about two-thirds of their adult size
and can follow the hen for long distances.

This juvenile male is already
practicing the mating dance that he
will perform the following spring.

FOLLOWING PAGE

Deep snow doesn't deter this male sage-
grouse in his search for food. He will use an
elongated middle toe to dig through the snow
to reach sagebrush. Sage-grouse flourish in
snow, often gaining weight over winter.

Wildlife have various ways to adapt to the cold conditions winter brings to sagebrush country. Mule deer (left), protected by thick coats, endure winds of thirty-to-forty miles per hour. The pronghorn (below) is the fastest mammal in North America; it can escape predators by running fifty-five miles per hour even in deep snow.

The coat of the jackrabbit will change to white to camouflage it against the snow.

Sagebrush and snow sustain sage-grouse throughout the winter. The birds search out energy-laden leaves at the tips of branches or dig below the surface. Their excavations can result in a warm refuge during a cold winter night.

Sage-grouse wings leave an imprint on the snowy sagebrush
steppe (above). The birds flock together during the
winter (right), sometimes numbering in the hundreds.

Fine, comb-like hairs on the feet function like snowshoes, enabling sage-grouse to walk on top of the snow. While other wildlife may starve in harsh conditions, sage-grouse can thrive in winter, as long as there is enough sagebrush and snow to provide for food and water.

Phillip Street checks on a nest of
newly hatched eggs in Nevada.

Datasets and Super Hens

Phillip Street, PhD candidate, University of Nevada, Reno

My passion for grouse research began in Gunnison, Colorado. I was a field biologist investigating the population dynamics of the Gunnison sage-grouse, which had recently been recognized as a separate species from the greater sage-grouse. As I began to understand how different components of sage-grouse life history influence populations as a whole, I also began to realize the difficulties of quantifying these factors to influence effective management.

Motivated by my fieldwork on Gunnison sage-grouse, I began a graduate degree program at Colorado State University, where I learned how to translate data into tangible results, such as probability of survival over time, and relate these data to changes in the environment. After that, I began my PhD work, investigating the effects of grazing by livestock and feral horses on sage-grouse in northern Nevada and southern Oregon. This high-elevation desert is characterized by cold winters and hot, dry summers. Sage-grouse, livestock, and feral horses all need water to survive on this landscape. Some of the most negative habitat impacts of grazing are observed around sources of water when the rest of the landscape is dry.

In order to quantify the relationship, my colleagues and I knew that we would need a robust dataset. One important driver for sage-grouse populations is chick survival. Building on techniques developed by other researchers, we devised a method that would allow us to count and monitor chicks without having to mark them, thus lessening risks to their survival.

The information we gather on chick survival also allows us to track rates of adoption. It has been known for some time that sage-grouse will adopt chicks from another mother, but the drivers behind these adoptions are poorly understood. There is also a great deal of individual variation among hens. Some mothers in our dataset never successfully raised a brood, while others, "super hens," raised a brood almost every year. We believe that these adoptions may play a key role in maintaining the genetic diversity within and among populations. As we begin to relate habitat to these important population drivers, we will provide this information to managers, and they will be able to make informed decisions about feral horses and livestock grazing rates on public lands.

Chick survival is an important factor in maintaining stable sage-grouse populations.

Whether it is working all night to trap the birds, waking at one o'clock to get to the hens while they are still brooding, or completing a vegetation plot in the heat of the Nevada desert summer, the work is challenging. It really becomes more of a lifestyle than a job. A typical day during the field season may be ten to twenty hours long. Unlike many other jobs, we do not return home to a house in a town or city. We live in primitive bunkhouses and field camps that are very remote. The nearest grocery store is an hour and a half drive on primitive roads.

Without passion and dedication, it is not something anyone can easily do. My technicians work selflessly to collect the data, and that motivates me to keep going. We know what is affecting the birds because we live with them. If what we learn can help inform management and ultimately help protect sage-grouse and enhance the Great Basin ecosystem, then it will all be worth it.

Saving the Icon of the West

Sage-grouse are one of many "sagebrush obligate" species: they depend on sagebrush and its associated habitat for existence. Protecting sage-grouse habitat also protects pygmy rabbits, sagebrush lizards, pronghorns, mule deer, and almost 300 species of birds.

A sage-grouse tail feather rests on top of sagebrush as a
storm gathers on the horizon. The population of sage-grouse
has diminished drastically over the past few decades. Today,
fewer than 400,000 sage-grouse remain in eleven states and
two Canadian provinces, and their future remains uncertain.

IF YOU RECALL HEARING A TREMENDOUS
"whoosh," followed by a gust of wind, back in September 2015,
you may have heard the collective sigh of relief as the U.S. Fish
and Wildlife Service declined to put the greater sage-grouse on
the Endangered Species List. The decision came as the result
of a court order challenging the USFWS's announcement in
2010 that including the sage-grouse on the list was "warranted
but precluded." In other words, the bird deserved Endangered
Species Act protection, but the agency had decided to devote its
limited resources to other species, such as the 1,200 species that
need recovery plans and the 250 candidate species awaiting a
determination.

What was at stake was about 150 million acres of sagebrush
habitat in eleven states, about half of the sage-grouse's historic
range. What is left is crisscrossed by roads, fences, ranches,
and gas and oil extraction infrastructure. The bird population,
which once numbered in the millions, is now estimated at
between two hundred thousand and four hundred thousand.
A study commissioned by the Pew Charitable Trusts in 2014
concluded that sage-grouse populations had declined by 56
percent between 2007 and 2013.

Signed into law in 1973, the Endangered Species Act aims to reverse
the extinction of plant and animals species caused by economic growth
"untempered by adequate concern and conservation," declaring the species "of
esthetic, ecological, educational, historical, recreational, and scientific value to
the Nation and its people." It typically works by limiting or eliminating the
development that is causing the plant's or animal's demise, an action that often
provokes intense passion in developers and environmentalists.

When the spotted owl was ESA listed in 1990, as a famous example, timber
production on federal lands in the Pacific Northwest was severely curtailed,
much to the dismay of loggers and the communities that depended on it. The
spotted owl hovered over political debates that raged regarding sage-grouse.
"Remember the economic impact of the spotted owl?" said the Colorado
congressman Cory Gardner in 2014. "The sage-grouse has seven times
the acreage of the spotted owl. You are looking at billions of dollars in lost
economic activity, millions of dollars in lost state and local revenues, and tens
of thousands of jobs lost."

A Feathered Political Football

Sage-grouse supporters are disheartened to see the bird become a feathered
football in a game of partisan politics. Environmental concerns had once
enjoyed bipartisan support: Theodore Roosevelt oversaw the expansion of
the national park system, and Richard Nixon created the Environmental
Protection Agency and signed the Endangered Species Act. And well before

Survival of young chicks depends on their mother's
protection and assistance in finding food and water.

politicians clashed over sage-grouse in the halls of Congress, citizens of all
political persuasions and professions were quietly taking action to protect the
grouse while forestalling the need to list it as endangered.

In the mid-1990s, sage-grouse populations sank to a new low, raising the
anxiety levels of the state and federal wildlife managers who monitor them.
The wildlife managers knew sage-grouse were in trouble, and they knew the
reason: loss of habitat. The Western Association of Fish and Wildlife Agencies
encouraged member states to create grouse conservation plans. The habitat
loss was due to a number of factors, most with economic implications. It
wasn't until energy development in all its forms spread into the Sagebrush
Sea with the ferocity of a wildfire that the concerns of grouse supporters got
national attention. With the possibility of ESA listing looming, the governor
of Wyoming, a state that is rich in resources such as oil, natural gas, uranium,
low-sulfur coal, and wind as well as sage-grouse populations, took the
unprecedented step of issuing an executive order to protect core areas of sage-
grouse habitat in August 2008. This set in motion plans to protect sage-grouse
that would soon be copied by other states.

A group of scientists led by Kevin Doherty, now of the U.S. Fish and
Wildlife Service, used data about lek locations and counts accumulated
from fish and wildlife departments to draw five-mile buffers around leks,
including nesting areas. "The maps showed important places for grouse and
included human developments, too," said Tom Christiansen, sage-grouse

The whole approach is based on cooperative, locally led conservation. It involves sitting down at a table and talking about mutual objectives. There are differences that come up, but you have to just talk through them and focus on common goals. That's the basis of a civil society.

—Duane Coombs

Tom Christiansen, Wyoming Game and Fish sage-grouse coordinator, releases a male sage-grouse at sunrise. The bird was captured as part of a population research project.

program coordinator for the Wyoming Game and Fish Department. "Roads, mines, coal, gas, towns, also natural features—even areas that already had environmental impact statements for potential development under way—this was all put together and mapped, and that's how the core areas were drawn." The core areas limit surface disturbance to 5 percent (on average) of each square mile and ban activity within six-tenths of a mile from a lek.

In Wyoming, core areas protect over 80 percent of the sage-grouse population, according to Christiansen. "Protection doesn't mean that nothing happens in those areas. There can still be wells drilled, just not dense well fields. Density and disturbance thresholds have to be met. Core areas are not refuges—they cover almost a quarter of the state of Wyoming. But we're trying to maintain development below the threshold that science shows has an impact on the birds." Time will tell whether core areas are effective habitat protection for sage-grouse. Population cycles and a harsh, dry environment that is slow to respond to management make measuring success difficult. And success, Christiansen said, is having sustainable populations of sage-grouse in the future. "I would never say the purpose of core areas was to avoid listing sage-grouse," he said. "The purpose was to avoid *the need* to list them."

The Sage-Grouse Initiative

Montana followed Wyoming's example in 2010 by identifying and restricting development in areas that contained 75 percent of the state's remaining grouse.

Other states soon followed suit, anxious that development would be curtailed if ESA listing became a reality. In Idaho, a controversial $700 million wind farm project with 170 turbines was suspended, then completely withdrawn in 2014, when development partners decided to redirect effort and capital to less uncertain projects. Wind farms, while applauded as an alternative to fossil fuel, are thought to disrupt sage-grouse mating and nesting because of their noise, movement, and potential perching sites for predators.

The Natural Resources Conservation Service, part of the U.S. Department of Agriculture, became a major player in sage-grouse conservation when it developed conservation plans friendly to sagebrush and grouse with ten ranchers near Roundup, Montana, persuading them that what was good for the grouse was good for the grass and the cattle that grazed it. Monetary incentives helped, too. When the Roundup effort showed some success, the agency extended the approach to Montana's other core areas and then to the ten grouse states, launching the Sage Grouse Initiative in 2010.

The Sage Grouse Initiative receives funding from the Farm Bill through 2018. More than $425 million have been spent on projects involving thirteen hundred ranchers who comply with conservation easements to preserve grouse habitat on their land. The initiative has reduced the threat of invasive grasses and wildfire on 1.8 million acres, removed conifers on 457,000 acres, protected 451,000 acres of agricultural land, marked or removed 628 miles of fences, conserved 12,000 acres of wet meadows and riparian areas for brooding hens, and hired twenty-six field staff members—"boots on the ground"—to work with landowners for grouse conservation. Ultimately, it is expected to protect at least 18 million acres of land for sage-grouse habitat. "The whole approach is based on cooperative, locally led conservation," said Duane Coombs, a rancher and coordinator for the Intermountain West Joint Venture, an organization that coordinates sage-grouse conservation. "It involves sitting down at a table and talking about mutual objectives. Sure, there are differences that come up, but you have to just talk through them and focus on common goals. That's the basis of a civil society."

This group of sage-grouse returned to their traditional strutting ground in Wyoming to find it had been turned into an oil field road. Traffic will disrupt their mating and the birds will cease to use the area. Research has found that chicks' survival rates go down, resulting in lower populations, as habitat becomes fragmented.

A sage-grouse family (above) encounters a highway during their early morning quest for food. Such a venture was fatal to this dead juvenile found on Highway 28 in Wyoming (right). Collisions increase during summer when sage-grouse have to move around to find food and water.

Desi Coombs, 12, (above) ropes a calf during the annual cattle branding on a ranch in Nevada managed by her father, Duane Coombs (left). A third-generation rancher, Coombs overlooks a vista of the Great Basin in Nevada.

What's Good for the Bird Is Good for the Herd

Jon Griggs manages Maggie Creek Ranch for the Searle family near Elko, Nevada. It is one of the largest cattle operations in the West, stretching forty miles north to south and twenty miles wide along Maggie Creek. The ranch is too large to qualify for incentives provided by the NRCS, but Griggs said conservation is at the core of its management philosophy. "We're in the business of raising high-quality cattle in a desert environment, and we know the best habitat for our cattle is also the best habitat for wildlife, so we do those things in common. Our best business model is to be good stewards for the land and the community." The sage-grouse is, he said, an indicator species of overall rangeland health:

While we have done a few things specifically for grouse, we manage rangeland for the best ecological site potential. When we achieve that, sage-grouse do very well. Specifically, we're real cognizant of where we build fences, and we use markers to minimize bird strikes. We're going to all-solar stock wells, and we try to limit availability of raptor perches. In the uplands, sage-grouse are doing well and expanding.

Newmont Mining Corporation is the largest U.S.-based producer of gold in North America. The company owns or manages almost two million acres of some of the best remaining sage-grouse habitat in the nation in the Great Basin of Nevada, stretching from the Sierras to the Wasatch Range. It also runs thousands of head of beef cattle on rangeland so vast it can be identified from space. For the past few years, Newmont has the distinction of having the lek with the largest documented number of males on it in Nevada—191 birds, a statistic range managers point to with pride. Jeff White is a rangeland ecologist and director of Newmont's land and cattle holdings. "Newmont has a land resource for which we're responsible," he said. "We try to do the right things by applying the best conservation practices on it, including managing for sage-grouse and other wildlife species." Newmont has undertaken one of the most formidable and complex challenges to healthy sage-grouse habitat: cheatgrass.

The invasive, volatile grass appeared in the West in the early 1900s and quickly outcompeted native perennial grasses and sagebrush, particularly in burned-over areas. Newmont, in conjunction with the University of Nevada, Reno, is experimenting with managed grazing patterns to take advantage of what cheatgrass has to offer while minimizing its impact on native habitat. Spring grazing on early-growing cheatgrass reduces it enough to give perennial grasses a chance to grow. Turning cattle onto cheatgrass areas in the fall reduces its standing dry matter and seed bank. In one experiment, fall grazing reduced cheatgrass biomass from seven hundred to eight hundred pounds per acre to sixty to eighty pounds per acre. "It's a very challenging set of practices requiring lots of monitoring and observation," said White. "We look at the timing and duration of exposure. It has to be done in combination with feeding supplements and water, and animals have to be concentrated in relatively small areas to have an impact on the cheatgrass."

Everybody's Favorite Whipping Boy

Both Newmont and Maggie Creek Ranch rely on allotment agreements with the Bureau of Land Management. Griggs expressed frustration with the slow pace of the BLM, which manages about a third of the land grazed by Maggie Creek cattle:

We have a really good relationship with the local office, but it's a challenge. It's kinda like doing business with the DMV. I work with really good folks, but it's a multilayered bureaucracy. For instance, the way we avoided listing sage-grouse is the BLM put out a land-use plan amendment that specified how they will manage public lands for grouse. The plan is four inches thick, and that's on top of existing plans. Navigating those things is kind of difficult.

University of Nevada students Lewis Mendive and Emily Harmon take samples of cheatgrass and other vegetation to monitor landscape changes. Their studies will help manage sage-grouse habitat at the IL Ranch in Nevada owned by Newmont Mining Corporation.

Without aggressive management, cheatgrass can quickly take over the area that was once healthy sagebrush habitat. Cheatgrass offers little to nothing to sage-grouse and other wildlife, and it contributes to volatile wildfires.

Junipers are being removed from southern Oregon and Nevada where lack of fire has allowed them to crowd out sagebrush and provide perches for sage-grouse predators. Researchers have found that sage-grouse populations can rebound once sagebrush habitat was restored by this method of management.

Sage-grouse are powerful flyers. They can fly 70 miles per hour in long, straight flights, and can often escape golden eagles and other predators with their airborne prowess.

Sage-grouse are no match for man-made barbed wire fences that cut across their habitat. Sage-grouse feathers with blood (above) demonstrate how hazardous the fences can be in open country. Fences cause high mortality for sage-grouse and are obstacles to many migratory wildlife such as pronghorn (right), elk, or mule deer.

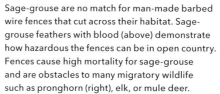

Steve Chindgren, a long time sage-grouse observer and falconer, places a reflector along a fence line to make it more visible to sage-grouse. The markers help improve visibility, but birds still succumb to unmarked or poorly marked sections.

Duane Coombs of Intermountain West Joint Venture works with the BLM to help implement that four-inch-thick planning document. "The BLM is everybody's favorite whipping boy," he said. "They get a bad rap. For example, they're supposed to manage the wild horse population, but Congress hasn't appropriated any money for them to do that. As a result, both the horses and the range suffer for it." The contentious relationships that supposedly exist between the BLM and private landowners have been grossly exaggerated, he adds. "There's this perception that Western ranchers are the same as those who took over the Malheur National Wildlife Refuge [in Oregon], but they were not legitimate ranchers at all. In my eighteen years of ranching experience, I would say 80 to 90 percent of ranchers move in concert with the BLM when it comes to range management."

Coombs acknowledges that BLM regulations are not well understood and that there is a widespread perception that the ranchers' needs are often overlooked by the agency. "Everybody gets frustrated and nothing gets done. Yet most of the problem is communication. We share a common vision—healthy rangelands and open space. These are the values we hold dear." He likes to use the example of his own family. "My dad was a cowboy, a rancher,

a classic Sagebrush Rebellion guy. But my daughter has grown up with conservation, seeing biologists at work, radio-tagging birds or whatever, so to her it's just natural that you would work to protect wildlife. I see a great opportunity to push forward a conservation ethic with this next generation."

Energy Drives the Debate

The love for the West's iconic wide open spaces is a common refrain in grouse country. For Erik Molvar, executive director of Western Watersheds Project, the Western ethos depends on open space and a lifestyle that includes hunting and fishing:

We want jobs and income, sure, but we want to be able to sustain the land we depend on, to work with it and not destroy it. When you look at the eastern United States, you see it's completely dominated by human activity. By contrast, the West is—or was—a vast area where you could see the landscape horizon to horizon uninterrupted by the hand of man. Westerners have a tradition that goes back to the 1800s to protect land and fish and wildlife. By caring for them, we ensure our own survival, too.

For Molvar, putting protections afforded by the Endangered Species Act into place to protect grouse was "a necessary safety net." Not listing the bird ripped a giant hole in that net:

The onslaught of gas and oil extraction in the early 2000s hit sagebrush country like a tidal wave. Listing the sage-grouse could have been a silver bullet to curb oil and gas exploitation, which just enriches a handful of executives while creating havoc with the planet. Instead, our addiction to fossil fuels continues unabated and may lead to the extinction of our own species.

The Pew survey mentioned earlier reinforces Molvar's observations where sage-grouse are concerned. A solid majority of residents in Colorado, Montana, Oregon, and Nevada indicated that protecting the sage-grouse was an

Cattle graze on public land in Wyoming. The Bureau of Land Management allows ranchers to lease public lands for grazing and works with them to conserve sage-grouse habitat.

Two wild stallions battle for dominance in Wyoming. Large wild horse populations in some areas of the West lead to concerns that they are overgrazing and causing damage to desert ecosystems. Others argue that sheep and cattle, which outnumber wild horses, should be reduced to make more forage available for native wildlife.

Heavy machinery has removed sagebrush and cleared the surface for gas exploration and drilling at Jonah Field, south of Pinedale, Wyoming (above). Jonah Field is the sixth largest natural gas field in the U.S. and it sits directly on top of one of the wildest and most expansive habitats for sage-grouse, now crisscrossed by paved highways and dotted with drill rigs and buildings. Many coal mines, like this one in the heart of the Red Desert area of Wyoming (right), contribute to the decline of habitat in the High Desert as well.

important part of preserving their Western way of life. The poll was conducted in response to the first sage-grouse protection plans written by the BLM, which Pew called a "mixed bag" because of their weak protections for the sage-grouse. Support from survey respondents crossed party lines, and rural voters were particularly supportive of grouse conservation efforts. A large majority (63 to 76 percent) of residents in the four states were in favor of stronger action by the BLM to protect sage-grouse and their habitat. "The poll shows support for the BLM to finalize scientifically based plans that strike a responsible balance between conservation and development," said Ken Rait, a director of Pew's U.S. Public Lands project. "Voters in the West from across the political spectrum, rural residents, and outdoorsmen want the BLM to safeguard this iconic bird and its habitat."

The proliferation of oil and gas wells across sagebrush habitat led to a 2.5 percent decline per year in male attendance on leks from 1984 to 2008, according to the *Journal of Wildlife Management*. Steve Chindgren, a falconer and long-time observer of sage-grouse, has seen big changes as well. As an example, he points to an enormous development in Wyoming's Green River Basin. Jonah Field, a vast tract in that basin, was destined to be developed for oil and gas extraction. He remembers the condition of the habitat back in 2006, when the draft environmental impact statement was prepared. "It was unbelievably wild and beautiful, the largest sage-grouse wintering ground in North America." He once witnessed two hundred males displaying on Sublette Lek. Now Jonah Field is the largest oil and gas development in Wyoming, crisscrossed by paved highways and dotted with drill rigs and buildings. "The habitat and the sage-grouse who lived there represented the best of America: wild, unbroken space that characterized freedom and all we hold dear."

It will never be the same again, Chindgren said, but that isn't the fault of the energy companies. "It's all of our faults. Our dependence on fossil fuels created the problem. It's up to us to moderate consumption and find alternative sources of energy." The scars of gas and oil development will be there for several lifetimes; Chindgren points out that even the wagon trails of the 1800s can still be seen on the landscape. And global warming, a result of burning fossil fuels, is changing the ecosystem in ways that are subtle yet profoundly consequential for all life, not just grouse. Molvar also suggests that there is evidence that the destruction wrought by fossil fuels goes beyond mechanical disruption of prime sage-grouse habitat. Climate change, if not addressed, poses a threat to all our habitats.

Tom Christiansen notes that cheatgrass is adapting to higher elevations and attributes it to climate change. "Thirty years ago [cheatgrass] was viewed as a problem limited to the Great Basin. Now it is widely acknowledged as a direct problem in many places, such as the Upper Green River Basin, at over seven thousand feet elevation." Additionally, annual cycles are changing—spring arrives earlier, frosts occur later, and the impacts of snowmelt are unpredictable and potentially destructive. West Nile virus was discovered in sage-grouse in

> The habitat and the sage-grouse who lived there represented the best of America: wild, unbroken space that characterized freedom and all we hold dear. It will never be the same again. It's all of our faults.
>
> —Steve Chindgren

2003 at an elevation of thirty-five hundred feet, according to Christiansen. Temperatures affect the viability of the virus. "When nighttime temperatures don't go below seventy degrees, the disease really gets cooking in the guts of mosquitoes," he said. "Sometimes we appear to have an altitude barrier to it, but I suspect it's more of a temperature barrier." According to the Centers for Disease Control, forty-four thousand people have been infected with West Nile virus since 1999. Nearly half of them developed brain or spinal cord infections due to the virus, and nineteen hundred people died.

Dealing with the vagaries of a changing climate in addition to declining habitat for grouse is challenging. "It all gets back to the word *sustainable*," said Christiansen. "When you have new information, you have to adapt and change. Don't get into lockstep. You have to be nimble."

An Uncertain Future for People and Grouse

Being nimble is difficult when so many groups and interests are involved in sage-grouse conservation. Add to that mix the new wave of so-called populism that has sparked a movement to return federal lands to the states and you have an even more complicated path forward. Currently, 64 percent of sage-grouse habitat is owned by the federal government, 31 percent is privately owned, and about 5 percent is under state control. Transferring federal land to the states would mean a tidal wave of change in sage-grouse habitat conservation.

The future is uncertain for public lands, but hunters, anglers, wildlife watchers, hikers, mountain bikers, climbers, and others who enjoy the outdoors have been outspoken opponents to removing lands from federal oversight. Jon Griggs said local and state governments don't have the resources to manage the land, and ranchers can't afford it:

At first blush, transferring land to the state has some attractiveness, but I don't know that the state of Nevada has the capacity to manage that much ground. I think that if it went to the state and if there was pressure to privatize it, ranchers would be left holding the bag. It would be attractive to lawmakers to sell it or make money from it somehow. Industries would have the first shot, then sports groups. Individuals can't afford to buy that land.

Erik Molvar (above), executive director of Western Watersheds Project, explains how sage-grouse require vast reaches of unspoiled sagebrush habitat to survive and how it is easily disturbed by industrial activities including wind farms and powerlines (above and left). Wind farms, while applauded as an alternative to fossil fuel, can disrupt sage-grouse mating and nesting because of their noise, movement, and potential for bird collisions. Molvar describes:

"This charismatic bird is an umbrella species and has become a prime indicator for the ecological health of the Sagebrush Sea. Protecting this one bird provides habitat for hundreds of other sensitive plant and wildlife species. As human activities degrade the health of Western lands, the sage-grouse disappear. If we want the sage-grouse to recover to healthy and stable populations, we must set aside the best remaining tracts of sagebrush habitat, and we must keep them free from further industrial destruction."

FOLLOWING PAGE

An aerial shot of Jonah Field, south of Pinedale, Wyoming, shows the scars left on sage-grouse habitat by gas and oil well pads. It will take several decades to a century or more for the land to recover and for sagebrush to return. Wagon wheel tracks from the 1800s are still visible in some parts of Wyoming today.

Field technicians Tom Correll and Rob Ritson catch two five-week-old sage-grouse chicks during a night trapping session to determine if a hen successfully reared her brood. If her chicks survive to thirty-five days, she will be recorded as successfully rearing her brood.

(Below) A five-week-old sage-grouse chick is weighed to check its diet and body condition.

A hen is equipped with a radio collar which allows researchers to monitor her and her brood movement throughout the summer.

North Dakota's sage-grouse are on the brink of extinction. Bird numbers plummeted from five hundred birds to just seventeen in less than a decade, not enough to support a viable population. A multi-state effort is under way to relocate birds trapped in Wyoming to North Dakota. Because of sage-grouse's site fidelity, such relocations have had poor success in the past. In order to improve the birds' chances, biologists are artificially inseminating females before relocating them, hoping their instinct to find a nest site will help them and their offspring adapt to their new locale. The study is designed to take two years. If the translocation is successful, it could help bring North Dakota's sage-grouse population to a viable level.

(Below) The head of a male sage-grouse is covered by a custom-made hood to minimize stress while researchers evaluate its semen, including checking sperm count and inspecting for the presence of contaminants.

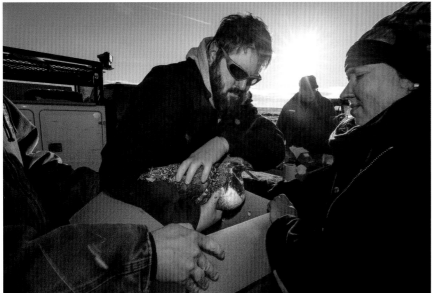

(Above) Biologists hold a hen on her back prior to insemination to improve chances of successful fertilization.

(Left) Birds are placed in individual boxes designed to house them during air transportation. Each bird is rigorously screened for disease by onsite veterinarians and fitted with a radio collar transmitter or solar-powered GPS transmitter to allow researchers to monitor movement.

(Bottom) Boxes that contain sage-grouse are placed onto a waiting airplane before being flown to North Dakota. The boxes minimize stress on the birds and limit their exposure to people.

Steve Chindgren is a falconer and long-time observer of sage-grouse. He said he has seen big changes over the years:

"The High Desert of Wyoming is one of the last strongholds of the sage-grouse. This land is magical and full of life. Many who speed along the roads through this Sagebrush Sea think there is nothing there. Sage-grouse represent all that is wild and unchanged. They live in one of North America's last tracts of undeveloped land; it is truly pristine wilderness. A feeling of sadness comes over me when I see stakes with red flags—meaning that this beautiful wilderness is slowly being turned into an industrial land. We can only blame ourselves."

Third-grade students and teachers from Little Snake River Valley School in Wyoming observe sage-grouse from a school bus (below). The grouse watching is part of an outreach program by Wyoming Game and Fish to expose local children to sage-grouse and the sagebrush ecosystem.

The White Rainbow

Steve Chindgren recalls waking up one late autumn morning in Pinedale, Wyoming, now a hub of oil and gas development, to discover that snow had fallen during the night—not an unusual occurrence at that northern latitude. He decided to take his falcon for a hunt on the new snow. Fog covered the ground and visibility was low, but he sensed that grouse were all around him. "I decided to just sit," he said. He could see blue sky high above him. As the fog began to lift, it formed a dense, narrow arch over the landscape. "I could hear the sound of wingbeats. The sound went on … and on … and on. It was a huge flock, or flocks. They took off, and as if they were one body, they flew under that arch. That was a spectacular moment for me—one that may only happen once in a lifetime. The phenomenon of the arch, the White Rainbow, has been known to recur, but not very often."

Rachel Carson saw an open book. Wilson Wewa heard the clicks and pops of a bird revered by his people. Jay Tanner saw a golden eagle take a sage-grouse in midflight. Steve Chindgren saw hundreds of grouse fly under a white rainbow in the sky. And thousands of people, throughout the ages, have witnessed the spectacular mating dance unique to the Sagebrush Sea.

People have coexisted with sage-grouse for millennia. Will future generations recall the thrill of sunrise on a lek or the sight of a flock of grouse taking flight? Will we be able to save these extraordinary birds that have been celebrated as the icon of the west for future generations? We don't know the answer, but we can continue to hope. It will take the deep commitment and dedication of people like the ones in this book who conserve sage-grouse and their habitat, and the care and understanding of more people like you and me.

Unless someone like you cares a whole awful lot, nothing is going to get better. It's not.

—Dr. Seuss

A group of sage-grouse gather beneath a "white rainbow" on a spring morning in Wyoming. This rare phenomenon occurs when an arch or bow is produced by the tiny water droplets of fog. The smaller droplets transmit light differently than the raindrops that create its more colorful cousin, the rainbow.

Photo Information

Front cover: Canon EOS 1D II
Canon EF 600mm lens
Canon 1.4 X teleconverter
1/320 sec at f/6.3, ISO 800

Page 2-3: Canon EOS 1DX
Canon EF 100-400mm lens
1/1250 sec at f/5.6, ISO 800

Page 6-7: Canon EOS 1DX
Canon EF 16-35mm lens
1/30 second at f/8, ISO 800

Page 8-9: Canon EOS 1DX
Canon EF 70-200mm lens
1/60 second at f/8, polarizing and
neutral filter, ISO 1600

Page 10-11: Canon EOS 1DX
Canon EF 600mm lens
1/125 second at f/4, ISO 1600

Page 12: Canon EOS 1DX
Sigma 20mm lens
15 sec at f/1.8, ISO 1600

Page 14: Canon EOS 1DX
Canon EF 100-400mm lens
1/125 sec at f/8, ISO 1000

Page 19: Canon EOS 1DX
Canon EF 24-105mm lens
1/1000 sec at f/8, ISO 800

Page 20-21: Canon EOS 7D II
Canon EF 600mm lens
1/4000 at f/4, ISO 640

Page 26-27: Canon EOS 7D II
Canon EF 600mm lens
Canon 1.4x teleconverter
1/800 sec at f/5.6, ISO 2500

Page 28: Canon EOS 1D III
Canon EF 600mm lens
Canon 2x teleconverter
1/500 sec at f/8, ISO 800

Page 29: Canon EOS 1D Mark IV
Canon EF 600mm lens
Canon 2x teleconverter
1/800 sec at f/11, ISO 500

Page 30: Canon EOS 1DX
Canon EF 17-40mm lens
1/5 sec at f/16, ISO 100

Page 32: Canon EOS 1DX
Canon EF 100-400mm lens
1/1000 sec at f/8, ISO 400

Page 33: Canon EOS 5DSR
Canon EF 16-35mm lens
1/125 sec at f/11, ISO 400

Page 35: Canon EOS 7D II
Canon EF 600mm lens
1/500 sec at f/11, ISO 800

Page 35: Canon EOS 7D II
Canon EF 100-400mm lens
1/500 sec at f/8, ISO 400

Page 36: Canon EOS 1D Mark IV
Sigma 14mm lens
1/20 sec at f/8, ISO 100

Page 38: Canon EOS 1DX
Canon EF 17-40mm lens
1/30 sec at f/16, ISO 400

Page 40: Canon EOS 5DSR
Canon EF 100-400mm lens
1/80 sec at f/11, ISO 400

Page 42: Canon EOS 5DSR
Sigma 20mm lens
1/250 sec at f/1.4, ISO 1600

Page 43: Canon EOS 1DX
Canon EF 16-35mm lens
4 sec at f/16, neutral density filter, ISO 200

Page 44-45: Canon EOS 1DX
Sigma 20mm lens
25 sec at f/2.8, ISO 2500

Page 49: Canon EOS 1DX
Canon EF 16-35mm lens
1/20 sec at f/11
neutral density filter, ISO 400

Page 52: Canon EOS 1DX
Canon EF 600mm lens
1/60 sec at f/10, ISO 800

Page 53: Canon EOS 7D II
Canon EF 100-400mm lens
1/2500 sec at f/5.6, ISO 400

Page 54-55: Canon EOS 1DX
Canon EF 70-200mm lens
1/80 sec at f/5.6, polarizing and
neutral density filters, ISO 1600

Page 56-57: Canon EOS 1DX
Canon EF 16-35mm lens
1/500 sec at f/5.6, ISO 800

Page 62: Canon EOS 1DX
Canon EF 70-200mm lens
Canon 1.4x teleconverter
1/60 sec at f/8, ISO 800

Page 65: Canon EOS 7D II
Canon EF 600mm lens
1/800 at f/4, ISO 800

Page 68-69: Canon EOS 7D II
Canon EF 600mm lens
Canon 1.4x teleconverter
1/800 sec at f/8, ISO 800

Page 72-73: Canon EOS 7DII
Canon EF 600mm lens
Canon 1.4x teleconverter
1/1000 sec at f/8, ISO 1600

Page 75: Canon EOS 1DX
Canon EF 600mm lens
1/3200 sec at f/4, ISO 1600

Page 76: Canon EOS 7D II
Cano EF 600mm lens
Canon 1.4x teleconverter
1/400 sec at f/5.6, ISO 1600

Page 77: Canon EOS 1D II
Canon EF 600mm lens
1/100 sec at f/5.6, ISO 800

Page 81: Canon EOS 1DX
Canon EF 600mm lens
1/3200 sec at f/5.6, ISO 800

Page 86–87: Canon EOS 1DX
Canon EF 600mm lens
1/200 sec at f/4, ISO 1600

Page 93: Canon EOS 1DX
Canon EF 600mm lens
Canon 1.4 x teleconverter
1/320 sec at f/7, ISO 1600

Page 96–97: Canon EOS 1DX
Canon EF 70-200mm lens
1/2500 sec at f/5.6, ISO 800

Page 100: Canon EOS 1DX
Canon EF 17-40mm lens
1/60 sec at f/10, ISO 800

Page 102: Canon EOS 1DX
Canon EF 16-35mm lens
3 sec at f/16, polarizing and
neutral density filters ISO 200

Page 108: Canon EOS 7D II
Canon EF 100-400mm lens
1/800 sec at f/8, ISO 800

Page 110: Canon EOS 1DX
Canon EF 70-200mm lens
1/200 sec at f/8, ISO 800

Page 112–113: Canon EOS 1DX
Canon EF 600mm lens
Canon 1.4x teleconverter
1/500 sec at f/8, ISO 800

Page 115: Canon EOS 1DX
Canon EF 17-40mm lens
1/80 sec at f/16, polarizing filter, ISO 200

Page 118–119: Canon EOS 1DX
Canon EF 16-35mm lens
1/40 sec at f/11, neutral
density filter, ISO 400

Page 121: Canon 7D II
Canon EF 600mm lens
Canon 1.4x teleconverter
1/2500 sec at f/5.6, ISO 400

Page 125: Canon 7D II
Canon EF 600mm lens
Canon 1.4x teleconverter
1/1250 sec at f/11, ISO 800

Page 130-131: Canon 7D II
Canon EF 600mm lens
Canon 1.4x teleconverter
1/5000 sec at f/8, ISO 800

Page 132: Canon EOS 1DX
Canon EF 100-400mm lens
1/2500 sec at f/8, ISO 250

Page 133: Canon EOS 1DX
Canon EF 100-400mm lens
1/2500 sec at f/5.6, ISO 400

Page 137: Canon EOS 1DX
Canon EF 600mm lens
1/2000 sec at f/8, ISO 800

Page 138-139: Canon EOS 1DX
Canon EF 600mm lens
Canon 1.4x teleconverter
1/4000 sec at f/8, ISO 800

Page 144: Canon EOS 1DX
Canon EF 24-105mm lens
1/25 sec at f/11, neutral
density filter, ISO 800

Page 145: Canon EOS 7D II
Canon EF 600mm lens
Canon 1.4x teleconverter
1/2000 sec at f/8, ISO 400

Page 149: Canon EOS 1DX
Canon EF 16-35mm lens
1/20 sec at f/16, polarizing filter, ISO 400

Page 150: Canon EOS 5DSR
Canon EF 16-35mm lens
1/640 sec at f/11, ISO 400

Page 154: Canon EOS 1DX
Canon EF 600mm lens
1/3200 sec at f/5.6, ISO 500

Page 159: Canon EOS 7D II
Canon EF 600mm lens
Canon 1.4x teleconverter
1/500 sec at f/5.6, ISO 1600

Page 164-165: Canon EOS 1DX
Canon EF 24-105mm lens
1/1000 sec at f/5.6, ISO 800

Page 170: Canon EOS 1DX
Canon EF 16-35mm lens
1/5000 sec at f/5.6, ISO 800

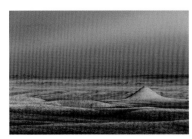

Page 171: Canon EOS 1DX
Canon EF 70-200mm lens
1/100 sec at f/11, ISO 400

Page 180: Canon EOS 7D II
Canon EF 600mm lens
Canon 1.4x teleconverter
1/125 sec at f/5.6, ISO 1000

Back cover: Canon 1 DX
Canon EF 100-400mm lens
1/250 sec at f/8, ISO 800

AFTER SPENDING MANY YEARS WORKING ON GROUSE, I knew my new task of documenting the life cycle and natural history of sage-grouse and their habitats wouldn't be easy. But I still underestimated the enormous challenges I was about to face.

To begin with, finding sage-grouse in the vast open landscape of the High Desert is nearly impossible if you don't know where to look for them. Spring mating ritual locations and their behaviors during that time are fairly predictable, but summer and winter seasons, when the birds become much more elusive and wary, are quite a different story. A hen and her chicks and even flocks of sage-grouse can easily melt into their environments. Without a doubt, many images in this book wouldn't be possible without help from people who know them best, including local observers, landowners, and field biologists.

Even after locating the birds, getting there is not an easy task. I drove as far as my car could go, then hiked in rough and steep terrains that are full of razor sharp rocks. Also I was often by myself in the middle of nowhere, far away from anybody or any town. Many of these remote places are so far out that simply getting a car stuck would mean many hours of hiking for help. But without disturbance from any light or sound, those remote areas—some of the darkest places in North America—were also among the most quiet and peaceful.

Another hardship was unpredictable weather. Sage-grouse live in a harsh environment where winter temperatures can dip well below zero with strong gusts of wind. Even springtime can turn into snow-blinding conditions without warning, and summer heat can soar to more than 100 degrees with a high possibility of severe thunderstorms. One time I was with a field biologist who was scanning the area for sage-grouse hens with a telemetry antenna. A thunderstorm appeared out of nowhere, and we had to run for our lives over uneven rocks with heavy backpacks.

Using a photo blind is a challenge itself. With conventional photography, photographers can move around to compose their image, but with a photo blind, my composition depends on where I set up my blind. Since I rarely photographed sage-grouse without some kind of blind—whether a portable blind or my vehicle—I spent as much time as possible scouting for a location. Sometimes this task took several days.

My photo blind served me not only as a shooting station but as sleeping quarters as well. I often had to be inside the blind way before dawn, typically around 2:30–3:00 a.m., so birds wouldn't be aware of my presence. During a full moon, however, sage-grouse will be out all night strutting on a lek, and in this case, I had to spend all night inside my tiny photo blind. Imagine rising early in the morning with the sound of male sage-grouse air sacs popping. The best alarm clock of all!

Patience is key to capturing good images of these elusive birds. I spent a lot of time waiting and searching for them. But there's a lot of planning and preparation to be done as well. I often pre-visualized potential images I wanted to capture, and planned and prepared as much as I could. There's a lot you can't control in nature photography, but I believe you should do your best to make your own luck. I rarely captured the image I envisioned. I'd be lucky to come back with any good images from a whole week of shooting. But when you succeed in capturing the image that formerly existed only in your imagination, it is extremely rewarding.

I usually carry the least amount of gear to get the job done. I often remind myself "less is more." Gear that I typically bring with me when shooting inside a blind includes a long telephoto lens (like 600mm with 1.4x or 2x extenders), a 100–400mm zoom, and a wide-angle lens such as 16–35mm. For landscapes, I rely on mid-range zooms such as 70–200mm and 20mm. I may bring some additional equipment for a remote control camera setting on special occasions. I have both a heavy-duty tripod and a superlight carbon fiber tripod for occasions when I have to make a long hike where every ounce counts.

Working on a book is challenging, but uplifting and rewarding as well. I believe photography is a powerful tool to raise awareness and inspire people. It can move people and change their emotions, opinions, and beliefs, by telling the stories of the animals people wouldn't otherwise get to see, so those voiceless animals that I have fallen in love with can be understood and valued.

Photo by John L Dengler / DenglerImages.com

Acknowledgments

Advice and Field Assistance

This book would not be possible without the support and assistance of many dedicated people who helped me day and night to make sure I achieved my goal of documenting sage-grouse and their unique habitat. I am also indebted to many friends who assisted travel plans, provided bird locations, or gave me much-needed advice on the book. Some offered hospitality in their homes or field stations, and some provided constant encouragement. With every step on this journey, I found warmth and friendship from people who were eager to give and share.

First and foremost, I would like to express my deep appreciation to my wife Monica, who has been the main force of this book, managing every aspect of it with insight and creativity. Her critical thinking, storytelling skills, and photo and story editing brought everything together. She taught me to be objective about my own images and helped me focus on the message. I am blessed to have her by my side.

I'd like to thank Kathy Love, for writing this beautiful story of the birds and helping me sharpen my vision by listening to my ideas and approach and stating them so eloquently.

Michael Schroeder, for articulately introducing readers to the sage-grouse and their unique ecosystem in the west.

John Dengler, my longtime friend and often field partner, for advice on photography and photojournalism ethics. He is not only a master of critical thinking but also a wise advisor, whether in the field or for photo visualization. His advice to "stay true to your image" helped me become a better photographer.

Steve Chindgren, for sharing his beloved place with me and showing me generous hospitality while I worked. Many of the images here would not be possible without his help. I'm forever grateful for his generosity and friendship.

Phillip Street, for his willingness to share his research with me. His long-term dedication to sage-grouse inspires me.

Jason Raymond LeVan, for taking me to the back county of the High Desert where sage-grouse spend their summers and being so patient with me even in areas infested with mosquitos.

Tony Mong, for taking me to places where my car couldn't go and getting my car out of the mud. He has saved me many times over the past eight years.

Christian Hagen and Andrew Olsen, for taking time from their busy schedules to accompany me in the Great Basin area.

Tom Christiansen, for his advice on sage-grouse's locations and for sharing his extensive knowledge of their behavior. I also appreciate him letting me tag along to document a historic sage-grouse artificial insemination and translocation project.

Erik Molvar, for his passion and dedication to informing people about urgent conservation needs and for letting me stay in his place multiple times even on short notice.

Duane Coombs, for his generous offer to let me tag along during the annual cattle branding in Nevada. It was a once-in-a-lifetime experience that I will never forget.

I owe gratitude to many people. I extend my sincere apologies if I have inadvertently overlooked someone.

Wyoming: Tom Christiansen and Tony Mong, Wyoming Game and Fish Department; Erik Molvar, Western Watersheds Project; Jason Baldes, Wind River Native Advocacy Center; Jason Raymond LeVan; Jeff Beck; Levon Big Knife. **Utah:** Steve Chindgren; Jay Tanner; Melissa Chelak and Kade Lazenby, Utah State University. **Idaho:** Steven Mathews, Idaho State University. **Colorado:** Jessica Young; Sandy and Bart Guerrieri; Tara Rowe, LightHawk Conservation Flying. **Nevada:** Phillip Street, University of Nevada; Duane Coombs, Intermountain West Joint Venture; Jeff White and Rhonda Zuraff, Newmont. **Oregon:** Andrew Olsen and Christian Hagen, Oregon State University; Jeremy Maestas, Sage Grouse Initiative; John Goodell; Wilson Wewa; Oregon Bureau of Land Management. **California:** Gail Patricelli, University of California Davis; Alan Krakauer; Ron Chilcote, Laguna Wilderness Press. **Washington:** Michael Schroeder, Washington Department of Fish and Wildlife. **North Dakota:** Aaron Robinson, North Dakota Game and Fish Department. **Wisconsin:** Greg Septon. **Oklahoma:** Steve Sherron and John Toepfer, George Miksch Sutton Avian Research Center.

Text Reviewers

Christian Hagen, Michael Schroeder, Steve Sherron, John Toepfer, Tom Christiansen, Phillip Street, Jessica Young, Gail Patricelli.

Book Staff

Monica Lee, Project Manager
Stephanie Thurber and Susan Ferber, Designers
Julianna Schroeder, Copy Editor
Pichai Chalachol, Illustrator
Josh Mitchell, Photo Prepress
John Dengler, Photo Advisor

This book is dedicated to the loves of my life, my wife Monica who constantly pushes me to be a better photographer and my daughter Evalyn whose gentle and loving soul and care for nature inspires me to be a better father and teaches me every day that all life forms in nature, even the smallest ones, are precious.